Women's Journey  r, encourage, and e y of Faith, Love and - person and online conferences and various interactive initiatives including teaching seminars, and fun, inspiring events.

WJOF is based in Saskatoon, Saskatchewan, but extends its reach nationwide through online media and traveling tours. WJOF is an interdenominational organization whose purpose is to gather, nurture, and discover the good news of Jesus Christ! The desire to see Jesus lifted up and encountered on a personal level is at the heart of all we do. You matter, and we believe God sees you and wants to connect with you.

 WJOF.COM

The Northern Initiative is an outreach of WJOF designed to empower women in the North through Christ. Our goals are to encourage the healing of hurts through Jesus, show genuine support, help build healthy relationships, provide resources and content that will encourage and strengthen women and their communities. We work to provide devotionals, blogs, interviews, stories, testimonies, classes, teachings, and workshops that are relevant to the needs of all women to strengthen their walk with God.

Northern Initiative
Introduction

One day, I was reflecting on the healings that Jesus has brought in my life since I surrendered my heart to Him. At that time, I was only about three years old in the Lord, and I was feeling quite confident about the healing that had taken place so far since I yielded to God. I thought, "Wow, I've come so far and have been set free from so many issues; I think I'm almost completely healed." I guess I was pretty naïve about my own heart and how much healing I needed because, in the next moment, I had a vision of an onion. The onion was positioned in the palm of God's hand, and I could see its multiple layers. I saw the Lord gently pull back a couple of layers from the outside of the onion while the remaining layers stayed intact. I knew God was showing me that there was still plenty of healing that needed to take place in my heart. Immediately I was filled with dread, frustration, and discouragement because I saw the reality of my situation. But, I know the Lord showed me this vision not to discourage me but to teach me that even though I was unaware of the depth of healing I still needed, He was gently restoring me. Layer by layer, He was changing me. I realized how unaware I was of my own pain, layers of trauma, and hurt He wanted to heal in me. I am so appreciative of how Jesus has taken my heart and ever so gently peeled back the layers and brought healing

Northern Initiative
Introduction

into my life. Now I get to experience peace, joy, and love in Him. I don't have to be afraid to face my pain head-on because the Lord gives me strength. I know I am in His hands as it says in Isaiah 41:10 (NLT), *"Don't be afraid, for I am with you. Don't be discouraged, for I am your God. I will strengthen you and help you. I will hold you up with my victorious right hand."*

Transformed by Love - Healing the Issues of the Heart

Day 1 - When You're Your Own Worst Enemy

> And you will know the truth, and the truth will set you free.
> John 8:32 (NLT)

One day, I drove to meet some ladies that I sat with on a board for a women's ministry. Our board consisted of four ladies, and I was the secretary. Over time, these ladies became friends of mine. On this particular day, I noticed that I was mentally preparing myself as I drove to my meeting by saying, "Okay, you can do this. You are good enough." There was almost a sense of dread in me. Then I asked the Lord, "What is this? Why am I feeling this way when I love these ladies?" There was nothing threatening about them at all. I realized that I was intimidated and insecure every time I came to meet with these ladies. Not because of anything they did or said, but I knew at that moment it had everything to do with my own heart and what I was carrying that was making me feel this way.

I heard this preacher man tell me one time, "Like many of us, there is a battle between our hearts and our minds. Your heart (the heart of God) can tell you one thing, and your mind tells you another." Up until this point, I didn't really understand what the preacher was talking about. At that moment, while driving to meet with these wonderful ladies, I realized that my mind was telling me I wasn't good enough to be sitting at the table with them. Two of the women were pastors of successful churches in the city, and the other was a smart, strong, insightful person, and she had a lot to bring to the table. In addition, all three were elegant and had so much knowledge and wisdom to share. So instead of being excited about what I could glean from these women, I sat at the table feeling small, less than, and intimidated. This is what brought on the dread. I knew that the way I was thinking was not the truth. I knew there was something in my own heart that needed healing. I thanked God for what He revealed in me and began to pray for the Lord to

Transformed by Love - Healing the Issues of the Heart
Day 1 - When You're Your Own Worst Enemy

> And you will know the truth, and the truth will set you free.
> John 8:32 (NLT)

shed some truth in my heart about these feelings

How many times, rather than facing what is in our hearts, have we run away? Instead of confronting these lies, we take the easy road and make adjustments in our own lives to stay in our feelings. We cater to these lies that we've grown comfortable with. Insecurity can rob you of where God wants to take you in your life. If you allow thoughts of intimidation and insecurity to control you, you could make decisions that alter God's destiny for your life. Sometimes we may have these feelings and thoughts unconsciously like I had about attending the meetings with the women's board I sat on. I was unaware of what was happening until the Holy Spirit showed me - He brought them to light. Allow God to confront these issues in your heart, and just as He set me free, He can do the same for you. You don't want to miss out on what God has for you because you can't confront the issues that hold you back. You will not regret facing them. It may be hard, but it's worth it when you find yourself walking in a new level of freedom.

Transformed by Love - Healing the Issues of the Heart
Day 1 - When You're Your Own Worst Enemy

> And you will know the truth, and the truth will set you free.
> John 8:32 (NLT)

Your thoughts...

Prayer Against Insecurities

Father, I ask You to heal me in the areas of my heart where I feel insecure. Help me identify the lies of the enemy that I have been listening to and replace those lies with the truth of Your Word and the truth of who You have called me to be. Forgive me for listening to these lies for so long that they have held me back from the destiny You have for me. I confront lies today and pray that You would make me aware of when they come to steal, kill, and destroy the plan of God. Help me deal with the issues of my heart when You bring them to light, instead of running away. Lord, help me walk in the freedom You have destined me to walk in. Thank you for revealing Your truth and setting me free from the lies. In Jesus' name, I pray. Amen.

Transformed by Love – Healing the Issues of the Heart

Day 2 - Perhaps You Were Born for Such a Time as This

And Mordecia had brought up Hadassah, that is, Esther, this uncle's daughter, for she had neither father nor mother. The young woman was lovely and beautiful. When her father and mother died, Mordecai took her as his own daughter.

Esther 2:7 (NKJV)

When you read the book of Esther, you will find a story of a young Jewish woman who became Queen over the fortress of Susa, reigning alongside King Xerxes. Esther was raised by her uncle Mordecai after her mother and father had died. There is no mention of Mordecai having a wife, so we can safely assume he was a single parent to Esther. Yet Mordecai raised up a great woman who became a Queen and saved her entire nation from being slaughtered. Mordecai was faithful to God and refused to bow down to Haman, the King's official. This made Haman so angry that he convinced the King to sign a decree to destroy Mordecai's entire nationality, the Jewish people. Esther's heritage was unknown to her husband, the King, so he had no idea he had signed off on his queen's death. The story goes on to tell us that Mordecai told the reluctant Queen Esther that she must approach the King even though she was not summoned. This could mean death for Esther if the King refused to see her. Mordecai then goes on to say to her in Esther 4:14, "Perhaps you were born for such a time as this." In the end, because of her boldness, Esther was able to spare the Jewish people from being slaughtered.

It doesn't matter what kind of family you grew up in. It doesn't matter how you came into this world. You may not have had a regular childhood, or the typical home, with both parents raising you, but I'm telling you that you can still grow up to be a mighty woman of God. Just as Esther influenced her nation by saving their lives, you can influence the destiny of others around you! I'm sure she had moments of self-doubt, where she may have thought, "Who am I to present myself to the King." But with the encouragement of Mordecai, she was victorious in her task to save her people.

Transformed by Love - Healing the Issues of the Heart

Day 2 - Perhaps You Were Born for Such a Time as This

> And Mordecia had brought up Hadassah, that is, Esther, this uncle's daughter, for she had neither father nor mother. The young woman was lovely and beautiful. When her father and mother died, Mordecai took her as his own daughter.
>
> Esther 2:7 (NKJV)

Currently, I am raising two girls who are not biologically mine. Presently, one is seven and one is sixteen. They are my relatives and came under my care through diverse circumstances. I always tell them, "You didn't come from my body, but you came from my heart." When I pray for them, I think, "Perhaps they were born for such a time as this." It doesn't matter that they are not born from a typical family; they will be great in the Kingdom of God. Just as Esther had a great destiny, I believe my daughters do too.

If you didn't grow up in a typical family or are currently raising your children on your own, know that God is for you. With God, you can succeed in everything you put your hands to. Like Mordecai, you can raise up an Esther to confidently influence nations and do mighty things in the eyes of our Father. Like Esther, you are lovely and beautiful. Don't be discouraged if you didn't grow up in a "normal" family or if you are not raising your children in a typical family. God has His hand on your life, and He will cause you to be successful in everything you do.

Transformed by Love - Healing the Issues of the Heart

Day 2 - Perhaps You Were Born for Such a Time as This

And Mordecia had brought up Hadassah, that is, Esther, this uncle's daughter, for she had neither father nor mother. The young woman was lovely and beautiful. When her father and mother died, Mordecai took her as his own daughter.

Esther 2:7 (NKJV)

Your thoughts...

Prayer for Influence

Lord, I ask You to help me be a godly influence to those around me, including my children and family. Help me pray for my children in such a way that I would call out their destinies. Let me see my children the way You see them. I pray they would grow up to be mighty women and men for You, influencing those around them and affecting the systems of the world for Your Kingdom. Help me understand that even though I may not come from what others consider a typical family, it doesn't disqualify me from being used by You. In Jesus' name. Amen.

Transformed by Love – Healing the Issues of the Heart
Day 3 – Creating Stability

> Then we will no longer be infants, tossed back and forth by the waves, and blown here and there by every wind of teaching and by the cunning and craftiness of people in their deceitful scheming.
>
> Ephesians 4:14 (NIV)

I used to make all my decisions in life based on my emotions and how I felt in the moment. If I got bored or uncomfortable, I would pick up and move, try to find a new job, or desire to start something different. I would constantly be looking for the next thrill or feeling of newness. When I became saved, I immediately felt this was something God was working on in me. I learned to hear the voice of the Holy Spirit and learned to submit to what He told me to do. I also learned to stay in difficult and sometimes uncomfortable situations regardless of how I felt. He caused me to be stable. He gave me the strength to endure and the power to be content in whatever situation I was in. He has shown me through the years how to be led by Him rather than by my emotions.

God created stability in me through the church I attended many years ago. The very first time I walked into that place, I fell in love with it. I could feel the love of God, and I loved the people. It was home. But then, down the road, I became bored and familiar. When things got hard, or I didn't agree with someone in the church, or I began to see the humanness of my pastors, I wanted to move on and go somewhere else. I sought the Lord about it, and He gently told me to stay, and I obeyed. There were many times I received job offers that could have easily caused me to be uprooted from the church and planted somewhere new, but I would always hear the Lord say, "Stay." Even though I felt like leaving, I stayed because I knew there was a greater purpose. As I listened to God and remained where I was planted, I noticed that I would fall back in love with the church all over again. Through my relationships in the church, God worked things out in and through me. If I had chosen to

Transformed by Love – Healing the Issues of the Heart
Day 3 - Creating Stability

> Then we will no longer be infants, tossed back and forth by the waves, and blown here and there by every wind of teaching and by the cunning and craftiness of people in their deceitful scheming.
> Ephesians 4:14 (NIV)

leave, I know that I wouldn't be where I am today. I stayed with my church family through the hard times, and it developed stability in me.

During this same time in my life, I started attending Bible College, intending to go for one year. Year after year, I would hear God say, "Keep on going," causing me to stay committed to my Biblical education until I earned my degree. This produced a lot of growth in my life, not just because of the knowledge I was getting, but because I trusted God to meet my needs, and He always did.

Being led by my emotions and the instability it brought was something I had dealt with my entire life. Sometimes it was hard to stay put, but the desire to uproot myself always passed, and I would be content again because I knew I was in the will of God. I just finished my degree last year. Because the church I mentioned early in this story ended up shutting down, I'm now planted in a different church. It was all God's timing. My emotions no longer rule me. Even if I'm confused, angry, or sad about something, I have learned to first go to God and pour out my heart to Him. I always ask Him, "What do You think or feel about this situation?" before I react or make any major decisions.

I wonder how many of us women, who can be over-emotional at times, make huge, life-changing decisions based on our feelings rather than seeking what God wants. We run from uncomfortable situations that can bring growth and build character. We seek happiness from external, material things rather than from the presence of God – the will of our Father. Emotions are fleeting, but God is stable.

Transformed by Love - Healing the Issues of the Heart
Day 3 - Creating Stability

> Then we will no longer be infants, tossed back and forth by the waves, and blown here and there by every wind of teaching and by the cunning and craftiness of people in their deceitful scheming.
>
> Ephesians 4:14 (NIV)

Your thoughts...

Prayer for Stability

Lord, help me not to make decisions based on my emotions. I know that as a woman, my feelings may tend to control my life. Help me to be stable in who You say I am. I pray that I will no longer be an infant tossed back-and-forth by the waves, but I will stand firmly on who You say I am. Help me to stay, regardless of my feelings in what may be uncomfortable situations, because I know that it may bring me growth. Help me to remain committed to the path that You have me on, and to be content in every situation because I know that it will eventually bring fruit. Thank you Lord that You are stable. You never change. You are the same yesterday, today, and forever, and I can rely on You in uncertain situations. Amen.

Transformed by Love - Healing the Issues of the Heart
Day 4 - A Girl Can Dream

> Never doubt God's mighty power to work in you and accomplish all this. He will achieve infinitely more than your greatest request, your most unbelievable dream, and exceed your wildest imagination! He will outdo them all, for his miraculous power constantly energizes you.
>
> Ephesians 3:20 (TPT)

Did you ever hear that saying, "A girl can dream?" I've heard it said many times in my life when someone mentions a goal they have, and it seems so huge of an idea to others that they quickly downplay it by saying, "A girl can dream." Don't ever dismiss yourself from good things. The enemy often comes and attacks your mind and wants you to dismiss the idea of the possibility that great things can happen to you! He wants you to stay down and give up on the possibility of ever having a better life. Satan wants to keep you down, and he does this is by constantly spewing lies to you, all day, every day. And when you even think about dreaming, he is quick to tell you how ridiculous your dreams are and how impossible they are to achieve. Sadly, we are often quick to listen to him.

How often are we quick to dismiss a dream that may have come from God? I have worked with youth for many years that have grown up the same way I did - in poverty, broken homes and with a mentality of hopelessness for the future. This is because they were never shown or told there was a better way. By working with young people from many communities, I recognized this pattern. They aren't used to their dreams being encouraged. They are scared because they've been disappointed so many times or do not possess the self-esteem to pursue their dreams. I remember encouraging them to pursue their goals and be hopeful about their futures, but the look on their faces would stun me. They had looks of confusion and shock that someone would tell them that their dreams could come true.

Perhaps you've found yourself in a place where you are no longer dreaming. Maybe no one has encouraged you in a long

Transformed by Love - Healing the Issues of the Heart
Day 4 - A Girl Can Dream

> Never doubt God's mighty power to work in you and accomplish all this. He will achieve infinitely more than your greatest request, your most unbelievable dream, and exceed your wildest imagination! He will outdo them all, for his miraculous power constantly energizes you.
>
> Ephesians 3:20 (TPT)

time, but I'm here to tell you that God wants you to dream! He wants you to expect great things in life. He has a great destiny for YOU! He wants you to know that He has good things in store for you. If you surrender your life to Jesus, He will be sure to bring great things to your life. You can have incredible adventures, great friends, fruitful relationships, and He will provide all you need to accomplish your God-given dreams! Will life be free from trouble? No! But I'm telling you God can open doors of opportunity that you could never have imagined! It doesn't matter how old you are, where you come from, or what kind of past you had; never stop dreaming those God-given dreams. When you allow God to come into your life, He can completely change the direction it's going. If you trust Him and step out when He tells you to, your life will be far from boring. God has great things in store for you! YOU, yes you! Regardless of what you may have been told your entire life or what you think about yourself, it's time to start dreaming again!

Transformed by Love - Healing the Issues of the Heart

Day 4 - A Girl Can Dream

> Never doubt God's mighty power to work in you and accomplish all this. He will achieve infinitely more than your greatest request, your most unbelievable dream, and exceed your wildest imagination! He will outdo them all, for his miraculous power constantly energizes you.
>
> Ephesians 3:20 (TPT)

Your thoughts...

Prayer to Dream Again

Lord, help me to dream again! Forgive me for dismissing myself from the good things that You have for me. Forgive me for allowing the enemy to speak louder than You. Lord, help me to know that You have great things for me because You are a good God. Heal me in the areas of my life that have caused me to no longer dream, that have caused me not to expect great things from You. I pray for areas of my life that have held me back from Your destiny and Your purposes. I ask You to help me walk in the destiny You have for me. I surrender my life to You today, and I accept all You have for me. In Jesus' name, I pray. Amen.

Transformed by Love - Healing the Issues of the Heart
Day 5 - Jesus Is There in Your Pain

> Once after a sacrificial meal at Shiloh, Hannah got up and went to pray. Eli the priest was sitting at his customary place beside the entrance of the Tabernacle. Hannah was in deep anguish, crying bitterly as she prayed to the Lord.
> 1 Samuel 1:9, 10 (NLT)

In 1 Samuel 1 and 2, we find the story of Hannah. It starts by telling us about Elkanah, who had two wives, Hannah and Peninnah. Peninnah had children, but Hannah did not; she was barren. Hannah greatly desired to have children. Her inability to have children took her into deep despair and anguish. By definition, deep anguish is one of the most painful emotions felt by humans. Other meanings are extreme pain or distress. It can encompass several different emotions, such as trauma, grief, sorrow, fear, and anxiety. The Message version of the Bible says, "...crushed in soul, Hannah prayed to God and cried and cried inconsolably."

Have you ever felt this kind of soul-crushing anguish? I remember being in the hospital with my mom in the days leading up to her passing. Death is nothing like in the movies. There we see images of the person taking their last breath, as their head falls to the side lifelessly and effortlessly, and that's where it ends. Hollywood did not prepare me for what I saw. I saw my mom in obvious pain and discomfort, fighting to breathe, right to her last breath. When she took her last breath, the look on her face mirrored such pain. Although I know she made heaven her home, I still had to get over the pain of seeing her suffer that way. Those memories were forever etched in my mind. In addition to that, I had to grasp the reality of no longer having her in my life, no longer being able to call her when I needed encouragement. She was the first one I would share news with, whether good or bad. She was my best friend, and she had an ear to listen. Her very presence brought me such comfort and strength. I didn't really know the impact of her love until it was gone. She didn't just say she loved me; she showed me. Losing her left my soul in anguish.

Transformed by Love - Healing the Issues of the Heart
Day 5 - Jesus Is There in Your Pain

> Once after a sacrificial meal at Shiloh, Hannah got up and went to pray. Eli the priest was sitting at his customary place beside the entrance of the Tabernacle. Hannah was in deep anguish, crying bitterly as she prayed to the Lord.
>
> 1 Samuel 1:9, 10 (NLT)

Many of us have experienced loss at some level, whether it be the death of a loved one, loss of a relationship or loss of a job. We may have experienced some trauma, grief, sorrow, fear, and anxiety like Hannah's deep anguish. But I'm here to tell you today, Jesus cares! God is concerned about what you've been walking through. And just as Hannah poured out her heart to the Lord, you can go to Him with your deep anguish. You can be real and vulnerable with Him. God will not be scared off or offended if we come to Him with our troubles and deep despair.

After my mom passed away, I stayed in the presence of God. I was both thankful to Him for walking me through this loss and just crying out to Him in the anguish and pain of losing my mother. He comforted me in ways I had never experienced before. He spoke truths to my heart about my mother and where she was. He walked with me through the darkest time of my life. Never in my life have I felt Him as close as I did in this season. I believe that just as Hannah received a breakthrough after going to God in her true feelings of anguish, we can too. God heard her prayers, and she left the temple in peace. We can leave the presence of God in peace, having poured out our hearts to Jesus. He will give us victory as He did Hannah. I know God was with me in my grief, and He will continue to walk with me, whatever comes my way, just as He will with you. Keep trusting in Jesus to heal you and bring you through your pain.

Transformed by Love ~ Healing the Issues of the Heart

Day 5 - Jesus Is There in Your Pain

Once after a sacrificial meal at Shiloh, Hannah got up and went to pray. Eli the priest was sitting at his customary place beside the entrance of the Tabernacle. Hannah was in deep anguish, crying bitterly as she prayed to the Lord.

1 Samuel 1:9, 10 (NLT)

Your thoughts...

Prayer to Heal Anguish

Lord, I pray that You would heal me in the areas where I have this feeling of deep anguish, whether it was brought on by grief, loss, or trauma. Please come into my despair with Your peace, Your comfort, and Your strength. I thank You, Father, that You care for me and that I can come to You in my anguish, and You hear my cry. As I pour out my heart to You today, Lord, I ask You to bring peace and comfort. Help me stay in Your presence when my heart breaks because I know that is where I can receive healing. Thank You for giving me victory just as You did for Hannah, and I trust You to bring healing to my pain. Amen!

Transformed by Love - Healing the Issues of the Heart
Day 6 - Overcoming Jealousy and Pride

> Since we are living by the Spirit, let us follow the Spirit's leading in every part of our lives. Let us not become conceited, or provoke one another, or be jealous of one another.
>
> Galatians 5:25, 26 (NLT)

Some years ago, I was a part of a very small church with a congregation of about fifty people. During this time, I served there as a praise & worship leader. I was the only consistent worship leader there, and I led every Wednesday and Sunday each week for quite some time. A couple had just moved into the city, and they decided to join the church. The wife and her husband were both worship leaders. When she came on board to help in this area, I was blown away by her voice and the anointing she had. When she led praise and worship, the congregation would be so engaged. They would be dancing, crying, and worshipping with their whole hearts. This was something I had rarely seen during my time there. As I stood there singing with her, I became jealous of her and grew very prideful. Often, after church, she would chat with me and try to make plans to hang out to get to know me, but I wanted nothing to do with her. I always had some excuse to blow her off so I could go home and wallow in self-pity because the congregation didn't respond to my worship the way they did to hers. I would think things like, "Well, the church doesn't need me anymore. I should just stop attending." I laugh as I write this now, but that was my heart toward her and the church.

One of these times, after an evening service, I went home, and I felt an overwhelming conviction and this ugly feeling in the pit of my stomach. I knew that the way I was acting was not pleasing to God. I went down on my knees that night and repented of my feelings and actions, and asked Jesus to help me walk in love. The following week, I opened my heart and life to this lady. Over the years, she taught me things about praise and worship that I hadn't known before. In fact, she taught me so

Transformed by Love - Healing the Issues of the Heart
Day 6 - Overcoming Jealousy and Pride

> Since we are living by the Spirit, let us follow the Spirit's leading in every part of our lives. Let us not become conceited, or provoke one another, or be jealous of one another.
>
> Galatians 5:25, 26 (NLT)

much more than I could have ever imagined. I believe she helped me get to the next level in my relationship with the Lord. She continually poured into my life, and to this day, she remains one of my closest friends. I often think about how the entire situation worked out and what I could have missed out on if I had stayed jealous and full of self-pity. I would have missed the opportunity to be free of jealousy and pride, and I would have missed out on one of the most wonderful friendships I have ever had. But because I followed the leading of the Spirit and humbled myself, I stayed in the will of God. Her ministry and friendship bless me to this day.

Transformed by Love - Healing the Issues of the Heart
Day 6 - Overcoming Jealousy and Pride

> Since we are living by the Spirit, let us follow the Spirit's leading in every part of our lives. Let us not become conceited, or provoke one another, or be jealous of one another.
>
> Galatians 5:25, 26 (NLT)

Your thoughts...

Prayer for Overcoming Jealousy and Pride

Father, please heal me in the areas where I may have jealousy or pride. I pray that You would bring these issues in my heart to light. Even though they may be hard to face, I pray that You would help me to heal from these issues in my heart. Increase my sensitivity to Your spirit so I would know when something doesn't sit right with You. Lord, I ask You to help me deal with these issues so that they don't hinder the relationships You have for me that are there to build me up. Help me to continue to walk in Your humility. In Jesus' name, I pray. Amen.

Transformed by Love - Healing the Issues of the Heart
Day 7 - Breaking Intergenerational Trauma

> And now that you belong to Christ, you are the true children of Abraham. You are his heirs, and God's promise to Abraham belongs to you.
> Galatians 3:29 (NLT)

Saturdays are usually when I deep clean my home. I will clean out areas of the house that aren't cleaned daily, like closets, under the couch, those kinds of places. When you have small children in the home, we, as parents, know that they tend to stick garbage and toys where they don't belong.

The Holy Spirit seems to always speak to me when I'm cleaning. One of those Saturdays, as I was going about my usual cleaning routine, I decided to move the TV stand to see if it needed cleaning underneath. As I moved it, I immediately became frustrated because I found all sorts of garbage, toys, empty wrappers, glitter, and dirt. As all of this was exposed, I immediately regretted moving the TV stand and sighed, saying, "Why do I always have to clean up messes that aren't mine." Immediately, the Holy Spirit spoke to me. He whispered something like this to my spirit, "That's how it is. You are dealing with the baggage of generations before you. You are called to deal with issues that you didn't create to bring healing to the areas of your life that need it." At that moment, I knew that because I chose to say "yes" and deal with my baggage and allow God to heal my heart, my children and my children's children would be free and blessed.

Many studies have shown that intergenerational trauma is often passed down and could affect the biological chemistry of our DNA and, in return, influence our behaviour. If we come from families where trauma has resided for years, there may be areas where healing is needed to break the effects of intergenerational trauma. We need to break the destructive cycles that have been prevalent in our families for years. Some of us may have a lot of work to do. I often get this picture of someone hacking at a thick bush full of twisted thorns and branches. To grow something fruitful, we must first prepare

Transformed by Love - Healing the Issues of the Heart
Day 7 - Breaking Intergenerational Trauma

> And now that you belong to Christ, you are the true children of Abraham. You are his heirs, and God's promise to Abraham belongs to you.
> Galatians 3:29 (NLT)

the land and soil for seed, and that's hard work; so it is with our hearts. How deep are you willing to go? What keeps me plowing at the ground of my heart is my love for my children. I don't want them to struggle with the same things that I or generations before me had to. I'm willing to do the work so my daughters can enjoy the fruitfulness of the land. Yes, we are responsible for our own salvation, but there are traumatic effects that can be passed down and must be worked out. Ask the Holy Spirit to show you the healing that needs to take place in this season of your life. I believe the Holy Spirit will begin to gently reveal the areas of your life that you need to surrender to Him. You can be free, and that will bring freedom for your children. They will be able to enjoy the fruitfulness of the land that you have worked so hard to develop.

In Genesis 12:2-3, God made promises to Abraham in exchange for his obedience. He promised Abraham that He would make his descendants a great nation, He would bless him and make his name great, bless those who blessed him, curse those who cursed him, and through his bloodline, all the families on the earth would be blessed. These promises are still relevant today. In exchange for our obedience to Christ, our children will inherit the benefits and blessings of God. As we obey God, blessings will follow us and be passed to our descendants. We are God's children, and His promises are for us. When we start to know those promises and make better decisions based on the fruitfulness of God, our children will be blessed, and cycles will be broken. As we learn to live in the promises of God that fill the Bible, our children and everyone around us will also reap the benefits.

Transformed by Love - Healing the Issues of the Heart
Day 7 - Breaking Intergenerational Trauma

And now that you belong to Christ, you are the true children of Abraham. You are his heirs, and God's promise to Abraham belongs to you.
Galatians 3:29 (NLT)

Your thoughts...

Prayer to Break Intergenerational Trauma

Lord, as I allow You to heal the garbage in my heart, You also bring healing to my children. Thank You for breaking off all intergenerational trauma and all generational curses that I may not know I'm carrying. Thank You for exposing the darkness in my heart through Your light and revealing the destructive patterns in my life, so that I no longer struggle over and over with the same thing. Holy Spirit, thank You for showing me the areas of my life that I need to surrender to You. When I surrender, freedom and fruitfulness will come to my life and my children. Thank You, Lord, for the blessings You have given us in exchange for my obedience, and that my children will inherit blessings because of my decisions. In Jesus' name, I pray. Amen.

Transformed by Love – Healing the Issues of the Heart
Day 8 - Change Your Mind, Change Your Heart, Change Your Life

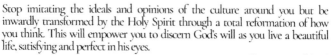

> Stop imitating the ideals and opinions of the culture around you but be inwardly transformed by the Holy Spirit through a total reformation of how you think. This will empower you to discern God's will as you live a beautiful life, satisfying and perfect in his eyes.
>
> Romans 12:2 (TPT)

The enemy loves to attack us when we are the most vulnerable, which is when we are children. When we're children, we can be told lies, and then they become "normal" thinking patterns that we take into adulthood. I had to recognize this truth in my life.

Lies, such as, "You don't deserve a good life. You are nothing. You'll never be free of this addiction," or "Who do you think you are trying to lead a good life?" were said to me again and again. So much so that they became ingrained in my mind, and I took them for truth. These lies could come from our parents, Satan, or any adult that may have had any value or influence in our lives. This kind of oppressive thinking is hard to overcome when it's ingrained in us from so young, but it is possible. The first step is to be aware of how you are thinking. Pray and ask the Holy Spirit to help you. The second is to replace it with the truth - the Word of God. Get the Scriptures planted in you so that your spirit will have something to fight back with when the enemy comes with lies. In Matthew 4, the enemy, Satan, tempted Jesus three times, and Jesus always came back to him with Scripture. If Jesus needed God's Word to fight the enemy, how much more do we? The Word of God will empower you to live the life that God has for you.

My mother was a residential school survivor. She experienced horrible abuse in that school and in her own home growing up. She was also in multiple foster homes for some of her childhood. For her entire life, she was repeatedly beaten down. She tried escaping the abuse and turmoil only to go into an abusive and toxic relationship with my father. He also had his

Transformed by Love - Healing the Issues of the Heart

Day 8 - Change Your Mind, Change Your Heart, Change Your Life

> Stop imitating the ideals and opinions of the culture around you but be inwardly transformed by the Holy Spirit through a total reformation of how you think. This will empower you to discern God's will as you live a beautiful life, satisfying and perfect in his eyes.
>
> Romans 12:2 (TPT)

own issues to overcome. My mother was in this relationship for many years. As I grew older, I recognized negative patterns forming in my life. As it was revealed to me by the Holy Spirit, I learned to change my thinking. I saw my life change because I changed the way I thought about myself and my surroundings by focusing on the truth of Scripture. As I ministered these truths to my mom and she read the Bible for herself, I saw her struggle to believe she deserved anything other than what she saw her whole life. It was so hard for her to change the way she thought of herself and the life that she deserved that I never really saw true victory in her life. But she never stopped believing that her children deserved a better life. It was easy for her to encourage us and speak life over us, but she couldn't for herself. I would have loved to see my mom healed physically, emotionally, and spiritually. Still, it didn't work out that way here on earth, but I know that she is now whole, healed, and in the most perfect state she can be in heaven. I also know that victory is for everyone, regardless of how hard life was or is for you. The promises of God are for everyone, especially if you have come from a life filled with all kinds of darkness. I want to encourage you with this. When you get God's Word in you, not only will you successfully battle against the enemy, but you will see healing and fruitfulness in your life!

Transformed by Love - Healing the Issues of the Heart

Day 8 - Change Your Mind, Change Your Heart, Change Your Life

> Stop imitating the ideals and opinions of the culture around you but be inwardly transformed by the Holy Spirit through a total reformation of how you think. This will empower you to discern God's will as you live a beautiful life, satisfying and perfect in his eyes.
>
> Romans 12:2 (TPT)

Your thoughts...

Prayer for Changing the Mind

Father, I thank You for exposing lies that may have been ingrained in me since childhood. Lord, I pray that You would help me overcome this oppressive thinking. Thank You for helping me become aware of how I am thinking. I pray that my thoughts would line up to Your Word and that You would help me speak Your truth to the lies that come against me. Lord, help me get God's Word in me so that when the enemy comes, I will know how to fight. Lord, help me to know that I deserve great things regardless of what lies I may have listened to in the past. Thank You that Your desire for me is to have a good life here on earth, full of Your fruit and Your promises. Thank You that Your promises for me are Yes and Amen! In Jesus' name, I pray. Amen.

Transformed by Love - Healing the Issues of the Heart
Day 9 - Waiting on the Promises of God

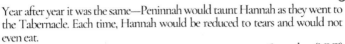

> Year after year it was the same—Peninnah would taunt Hannah as they went to the Tabernacle. Each time, Hannah would be reduced to tears and would not even eat.
>
> 1 Samuel 1:7 (NLT)

The enemy will taunt us by trying to get us to focus on what we do not have. He will remind you continuously of what you lack. Satan will try to get you lost in your pain, the desire, and the want of something so badly that you will lose your peace. I struggled with this for many years. Sometimes I would become so focused on what I was waiting for that I would lose my peace and become disappointed and discontented in the waiting. The enemy wants you to lose all hope and faith and stop expecting good things from God. We always need to have the confident expectation that the Lord will do what He said He would do, even if it's not in our timing. We may have our lives and timelines all mapped out, but the Lord has a different plan. We must learn how to wait and at the same time allow ourselves to enjoy life in the process. God has great things that He wants to accomplish in us now. Today, while we are in the waiting period, we can still be happy, content, and walking in our destiny. Whatever you find yourself waiting for, recognize that its fulfillment is not what brings you value. You are already valuable, just as you are.

In 1 Samuel 1 and 2, we find the story of a woman named Hannah who was barren. Both Hannah and Peninnah were married to Elkanah. I can imagine how Hannah felt – going year after year without becoming pregnant while Penniah continued to have children. Penninah tormented and teased Hannah about her inability to conceive a child. All Hannah could do was stand by and watch as the very thing she desired happened to someone else. Have you ever prayed and waited for a blessing only to see it come so quickly and easily to others? That is a true test of your heart. Maybe you've been waiting for a husband, or like Hannah, are waiting to have children.

Transformed by Love - Healing the Issues of the Heart
Day 9 - Waiting on the Promises of God

> Year after year it was the same—Peninnah would taunt Hannah as they went to the Tabernacle. Each time, Hannah would be reduced to tears and would not even eat.
>
> 1 Samuel 1:7 (NLT)

Perhaps you've been standing on the promise of God for salvation for your family. Or, it could be something like waiting for the call of God on your life to be fulfilled, having a home, or getting a job. And yet, just like Hannah, you may see so many others around you getting what you are waiting to receive. Ladies, in all of this, we must keep our hearts pure! I don't think we should give up on what we are waiting for either. Like with everything else, there needs to be a balance. Know and believe in the promise, go to God and remind Him of what He said, pray about it, and leave it there. Don't become so obsessed that it steals your peace or causes you to be discontent.

I have been single since I came to the Lord. I was in a relationship at that time, and the Lord told me this very shortly after I became saved. He said, "I have someone else for you." And I've stood on what He said since that day. Years have passed, and I have been a bridesmaid seven times since! That's right, seven times! In each wedding I stood in, I learned to celebrate them with my whole heart. I refused to allow the enemy to steal any more of my peace. I learned to be satisfied and content in the waiting. Do I have moments where it is hard? Yes! Do I have moments where I've been weak? Absolutely! But in all this, I know that God's promises will come to pass just as they did for Hannah. Hannah eventually did bear children, and she was able to praise God for her breakthrough.

Transformed by Love - Healing the Issues of the Heart
Day 9 - Waiting on the Promises of God

> Year after year it was the same—Peninnah would taunt Hannah as they went to the Tabernacle. Each time, Hannah would be reduced to tears and would not even eat.
>
> 1 Samuel 1:7 (NLT)

Your thoughts...

Prayer for Waiting on the Promises of God

Lord, I pray that instead of focusing on what I do not have, You will help me focus on the blessings I do have. I pray that disappointment will not overtake me, but I will continue to stand in hope and faith for what You have for me, even if it's not on my timeline. I submit to Your plans for my life, and I know that I can be happy, content, and walk in Your destiny even in the waiting. I know that what I'm waiting for does not bring me value, but I am valuable just as I am. Lord, help me celebrate with those around me as they receive what they've been waiting for. Help me keep my heart pure as I wait on the promises You have for me. I'll leave it in Your hands, Lord. Thank You for the peace that comes after I leave it in Your hands. In Jesus' name, I pray. Amen.

Transformed by Love - Healing the Issues of the Heart
Day 10 - An Abundant Life

A thief has only one thing in mind—he wants to steal, slaughter and destroy. But I (Jesus) have come to give you everything in abundance, more than you expect —life in its fullness until you overflow!

John 10:10 (TPT)

Are you living a fully abundant life? I'm not talking about material possessions or the riches of this world. I'm talking about a life so filled with the character and love of God that it creates favour, blessings, and the fullness of joy and peace in your heart. Do you have victory in your life, or are you struggling with the same battles over and over? Are the fruit of the Spirit evident in your life? Are you growing in your walk with God, gaining more and more victory as the years go by? Do you see miracles? Are you seeing your family and friends saved? Are you experiencing a life where God is taking you where you never thought you'd go? This is the kind of life Jesus desires for you! He wants you to be overflowing with His presence. He wants to not only meet your expectations but exceed them.

For many years, I struggled to believe that I could ever live an abundant life. I thought living this Christian life just guaranteed me entrance to heaven when I died. Until then, I just needed to make it through this wicked world somehow. When I began to read His Word, I began to see how God desired me to live an abundant life now, in this world, while I'm still living and breathing. Before I came to Jesus, I struggled for many years with depression. My outlook on life was very bleak, and I viewed everything through a distorted lens. My mind was always cloudy, and I had a hard time focusing. I always felt defeated and unhappy. No matter how many goals in life I would reach, it just didn't bring me happiness. One time in church, as I sat in my chair with my hands barely lifted during worship, I felt a weight lift off me. Such peace filled my heart, and I knew the presence of God did something in me. A shifting had taken place. I could think clearly, and I had this energy that I never had before.

Transformed by Love ~ Healing the Issues of the Heart
Day 10 ~ An Abundant Life

> A thief has only one thing in mind—he wants to steal, slaughter and destroy. But I (Jesus) have come to give you everything in abundance, more than you expect—life in its fullness until you overflow!
>
> John 10:10 (TPT)

I was filled with His overwhelming love to the point where everything in this world seemed insignificant in comparison to His presence. At that moment, I knew God had so much more for me than just taking me to heaven when I die.

An abundant life requires us to stay rooted in the presence of God, so we continue to be shaped and moulded by Him. We must allow Jesus to show us those things in our hearts that steal, kill, and destroy the plan of abundance Jesus has for us. In John 10:1-18, Jesus talks about the importance of relationship with Him. Relationship with the Good Shepherd (Jesus) will cause us to know His voice, and He will know ours, just as sheep know the voice of their shepherd. Sheep will not respond to a voice they do not know. In fact, they would run the other way. We will know His voice if we are His (Jesus), and He will know ours. We will believe what He tells us about the incredible life He has for us. And when we hear the enemy's voice, we will run the other way. The voice of Jesus will lead you into the abundant life that He has for you. If you do not know His voice, you can simply ask Him to come and be your guide, your Shepherd that leads you into the good things He has for you.

Transformed by Love - Healing the Issues of the Heart
Day 10 - An Abundant Life

> A thief has only one thing in mind—he wants to steal, slaughter and destroy. But I (Jesus) have come to give you everything in abundance, more than you expect—life in its fullness until you overflow!
>
> John 10:10 (TPT)

Your thoughts...

Prayer for an Abundant Life

Lord, I thank you for giving me an abundant life and that I can walk in all Your promises while I am here on earth. I thank You for the victory in my life. Thank You for the fruitfulness in my life. Thank You for the miracles in my life. I'm thankful that I can experience You wherever I am in life. Even if I'm walking in darkness, You will meet me there. I pray that when the enemy comes to steal, slaughter, and destroy Your plans, I will stand on Your promise to give me everything in abundance, more than I can expect. You'll give me a life full of Your Spirit so that I overflow. Show me if I have a distorted lens that is self-destructive. I pray that You would help me look through the lens of Your Word. Thank You that I walk in joy, peace, and love while here on earth. I pray that I stay rooted in You and Your presence as You shape and mould me. Show me the things in my heart that steal, kill, and destroy the plan You have for me. Help me to stay in a relationship with You so that I will hear Your voice and run from the enemy's voice. In Jesus' name, I pray. Amen.

Transformed by Love - Healing the Issues of the Heart

Day 11 - God Cares About Every Detail in Your Life

> What is the price of five sparrows—two copper coins? Yet God does not forget a single one of them. And the very hairs on your head are all numbered. So don't be afraid; you are more valuable to God than a whole flock of sparrows.
>
> Luke 12:6, 7 (NLT)

I remember these beautiful earrings that my mom wore. They were small, circular, with silver on the inside and had a black sparkle on the outside. They were very sparkly and looked so pretty on her. Shortly after she passed away, my siblings and I went through her things, intending to give her jewelry, clothes, and other items to family, friends, and charity. I was frantically looking for those earrings everywhere. I looked through every area of her bedroom. I hunted through her jewelry box a few times, the pockets of her many coats, the top of her bedroom closet, and I couldn't find them anywhere. Eventually, I gave up and thought to myself, "She must have given them away already," because that was my mom's nature. If someone liked something of hers, she was quick to give it away.

One Saturday, a few months after my mom's funeral, I woke up from a dream about her that made me miss her so much. I cried throughout the morning, thinking of her as I cleaned and went about my usual Saturday routine. Then I decided to clean the top of the fridge because I had noticed quite a bit of clutter up there. As I removed papers, old bills, and other clutter, I found my mom's earrings! Immediately I burst into tears as I held them in my hand, and I knew it was God's way of showing me that He cared about what I was walking through. I felt like finding those earrings was a little kiss from heaven. To this day, I have no idea how they got on top of the fridge or who might have placed them there. Maybe it was my mother when she visited before she passed. Regardless of how they got there, I knew that I was meant to find them at that moment. God knew what it would mean to me at that specific time in my life. Even if He set it up way beforehand, He knew what was coming. He knew the

Transformed by Love - Healing the Issues of the Heart
Day 11 - God Cares About Every Detail in Your Life

> What is the price of five sparrows—two copper coins? Yet God does not forget a single one of them. And the very hairs on your head are all numbered. So don't be afraid; you are more valuable to God than a whole flock of sparrows.
>
> Luke 12:6, 7 (NLT)

exact moment I would need His comfort in the future!

My sisters, I want to encourage you - God cares about every single detail of your life. He knows exactly how to comfort you, and He knows exactly what you need. In the Scripture above, Jesus was reminding His disciples that if He ensures the sparrows' needs are met, how much more will He care about the details of His children? He knows every detail of your life, including the number of hairs on your head. These small details are important to Him. We can trust Him with the details and desires of our hearts. We can trust Him to comfort us when we need comforting, counsel us, and guide us as we seek Him. We need not fear or be anxious about the future because God will be there with us, taking care of every need we have. As long as we trust Him, we can be sure that He is faithful and will always come through as the loving Father He is.

Transformed by Love - Healing the Issues of the Heart

Day 11 - God Cares About Every Detail in Your Life

> What is the price of five sparrows—two copper coins? Yet God does not forget a single one of them. And the very hairs on your head are all numbered. So don't be afraid; you are more valuable to God than a whole flock of sparrows.
>
> Luke 12:6, 7 (NLT)

Your thoughts...

Prayer for Taking Care of Every Detail of My Life

Father, I thank You that You care about every single detail of My life. Lord, whatever I care about, You care about too. You comfort me in my pain. Whatever is important to me is important to You too. Thank You that I can trust You with every single little need. I trust You with the details and the desires of my heart. I trust You to comfort me when I need comforting, counsel me when I need counselling, and guide me when I need guidance. I don't have to fear the future because You will be there with me, taking care of every need I have. Thank You for your faithfulness, Jesus. Amen.

Transformed by Love – Healing the Issues of the Heart

Day 12 – Finding my Identity in Christ

All praise to God, the Father of our Lord Jesus Christ, who has blessed us with every spiritual blessing in the heavenly realms because we are united with Christ. Even before he made the world, God loved us and chose us in Christ to be holy and without fault in his eyes. God decided in advance to adopt us into his own family by bringing us to himself through Jesus Christ. This is what He wanted to do, and it have Him great pleasure.

Ephesians 1:3-5 (NLT)

There was a time in my life when God stripped me down of everything I thought I was - what I had unknowingly built my identity upon. It was around my first year as a Bible College student. My daughter was a baby, and I thought I would take this time to build myself up in Christ by going to Bible College. Until that time, I had always worked, and I worked hard! I had built myself a reputation for being a hard worker. I would work from morning until night in every job I had after university. I wanted to make something of myself, and I thought having a career would do it. Because of my work ethic, I was usually moved to manager or supervisor within a few months of working in an organization, and I prided myself on that. During my first year of Bible College, I really learned to surrender my life to God, listen for His voice, and allow Him to lead me. I learned to trust His voice every time He spoke. I was careful to yield to every direction I felt Him leading me in and trusted Him with every decision He made for my life. Around this time, I found myself with no titles and very little money for the luxuries I was accustomed to having. Every need was met for my daughter, all my bills were paid, but I didn't have the extra money I was used to having. In addition to this, my car broke down, and I had to rely on my sister, who was my roommate, to take me where I needed to go. It was a very humbling time for me.

Spiritually, I was on fire for God, and I noticed that I couldn't laugh at the same jokes I used to when I was with my friends. The crude, vulgar things I once found funny were disgusting to me. I couldn't walk into the same places as before without

Transformed by Love - Healing the Issues of the Heart
Day 12 - Finding my Identity in Christ

> All praise to God, the Father of our Lord Jesus Christ, who has blessed us with every spiritual blessing in the heavenly realms because we are united with Christ. Even before he made the world, God loved us and chose us in Christ to be holy and without fault in his eyes. God decided in advance to adopt us into his own family by bringing us to himself through Jesus Christ. This is what He wanted to do, and it have Him great pleasure.
>
> Ephesians 1:3-5 (NLT)

feeling conviction. It was then I began to question, "Who am I? If I don't have titles, if I don't have money, nice vehicles, loads of friends, who am I?" At that moment, I realized my identity was built on all these other things, and when the Lord asked me to lay them all down, I didn't know who I was anymore. Little did I know this was exactly where God wanted me. It was a very vulnerable place to be. When I went places, people often asked me, "Where are you working now?" They gave me this odd look when I told them I was in Bible College. I think it was a look of confusion and a little bit of, "You're crazy!" It was a look that I got used to over the years. To them, I was the crazy Christian girl who gave up everything for nothing. It didn't bother me because even though I had barely anything, I was the most content I had ever been in my entire life because I knew I was in the will of God.

The Lord began to show me who I was in Him. He started to build me up into who He created me to be, and I found my identity in Him! In summary, Ephesians 1:3-14 says that we are CHOSEN, ADOPTED by Him, ACCEPTED by Him, and REDEEMED. He has made His will known, and SEALED us by the Holy Spirit. I began to meditate on these scriptures until they became ingrained in my very being. It changed my life. I was no longer defined by the world but by God's spiritual promises. I no longer felt the pull to please the world through titles, nice things and doing what others expected. I was free, and all I wanted to do was please my Heavenly Father. I prided myself in those worldly things, and God had to tear them all down. It was a challenging

Transformed by Love - Healing the Issues of the Heart
Day 12 – Finding my Identity in Christ

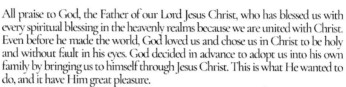

> All praise to God, the Father of our Lord Jesus Christ, who has blessed us with every spiritual blessing in the heavenly realms because we are united with Christ. Even before he made the world, God loved us and chose us in Christ to be holy and without fault in his eyes. God decided in advance to adopt us into his own family by bringing us to himself through Jesus Christ. This is what He wanted to do, and it have Him great pleasure.
>
> Ephesians 1:3-5 (NLT)

but meaningful lesson for me to learn.

Transformed by Love - Healing the Issues of the Heart
Day 12 – Finding my Identity in Christ

All praise to God, the Father of our Lord Jesus Christ, who has blessed us with every spiritual blessing in the heavenly realms because we are united with Christ. Even before he made the world, God loved us and chose us in Christ to be holy and without fault in his eyes. God decided in advance to adopt us into his own family by bringing us to himself through Jesus Christ. This is what He wanted to do, and it have Him great pleasure.

Ephesians 1:3-5 (NLT)

Your thoughts...

Prayer for Identity in Jesus

Father, I thank you for stripping down the identity that I have unknowingly built for myself. Lord, forgive me for identifying myself with the things of this world. As I surrender my life to You, I pray that You would build me up into who You say I am. I pray that I will yield to every direction that You are leading me in, and I will trust You with every decision You make for my life. Thank You that I do not have to build my identity on the expectations of others or this world. Build me up in who You are and help me to accept Your love. Help me know that I am chosen, and I am a daughter of God, redeemed and sealed by Your Holy Spirit. Thank You for changing my life so that I am no longer pulled to please the world by titles and other people's expectations, but I am pulled to please You, my Heavenly Father. Amen.

Transformed by Love - Healing the Issues of the Heart
Day 13 – God's Plan for You

> For I know the plans I have for you," says the Lord. "They are plans for good and not for disaster, to give you a future and a hope. In those days when you pray, I will listen. If you look for me wholeheartedly, you will find me.
>
> Jeremiah 29:11-13 (NLT)

Jeremiah was an Old Testament prophet. In the Scriptures above, he encouraged and comforted his people, the Israelites, who had been deported from Jerusalem and forcibly taken to Babylon, a foreign country. In what may have felt like a hopeless situation, Jeremiah encouraged the Israelites to make the best of the circumstances and environment in which they found themselves. He also reminded them that God still heard their prayers and that the Lord had a great destiny for them. Although the future looked bleak, they could lean on God's promise that He had their outcome in His hands. He promised to eventually return them to their homelands.

Growing up in a Northern Community in Saskatchewan, isolation was very much something that I was familiar with. In addition to the remote location of our First Nation, I grew up in an area of the reserve that was isolated from the rest of the community. Our family rarely had reliable transportation to get around the reserve, so sometimes, I would go the entire summer without seeing my friends from school. Internet wasn't even around yet, and only two people in the whole community had land-line phones. Therefore, communication with the outside world was not an option either. Sometimes I would go days without seeing anyone besides the faces of my siblings and parents, which I grew used to. Sometimes the isolation felt overwhelming. Late at night, when the radio stations had a crystal-clear signal, I would turn the dial through the stations to listen to people speaking in different languages. It comforted me to know other people were out there in the world, living their lives.

Transformed by Love - Healing the Issues of the Heart
Day 13 - God's Plan for You

> For I know the plans I have for you," says the Lord. "They are plans for good and not for disaster, to give you a future and a hope. In those days when you pray, I will listen. If you look for me wholeheartedly, you will find me.
> Jeremiah 29:11-13 (NLT)

I tell you all of this because I want you to know I understand what it's like to feel so isolated, so alone - forgotten. I know what it's like to feel hopeless, to wonder if you will ever get out or if anything will ever change. There were moments when it felt difficult to even hope about the future. I would often wonder what my purpose was or if there was any purpose at all. Maybe you didn't choose your current environment but were born into it, and you haven't even realized that you carried some of these feelings. Even more problematic is if there are uncomfortable conditions in addition to the isolation, such as overcrowded housing, not enough food to go around, or addicted family members. I know it can feel defeating because I faced all these things while growing up in my home community as an Indigenous person. But I want to encourage you today with the truth! Whether you currently find yourself in this environment or if you have grown up this way, there is hope through Christ. If you haven't yet found peace, I want to tell you that you can have peace in Jesus. You can stand on the promises of God today! Like what it states in Jeremiah 29:11, God has a great future for you, and through Him, there is so much hope, peace, and comfort. You can find purpose in Him. You can fulfill unimaginable dreams through Him! I want to invite you today to stand on this Word - these Scriptures in whatever circumstance you face today. Just like when Jeremiah gave strength to the Israelites in what seemed like a hopeless time for them, Jesus wants to give you hope. Real hope that promises you a great future is attainable!

Transformed by Love - Healing the Issues of the Heart
Day 13 – God's Plan for You

For I know the plans I have for you," says the Lord. "They are plans for good and not for disaster, to give you a future and a hope. In those days when you pray, I will listen. If you look for me wholeheartedly, you will find me.

Jeremiah 29:11-13 (NLT)

Your thoughts...

Prayer Against Hopelessness

Lord, I pray against all the hopelessness, loneliness, and isolation I may feel. Jesus, I thank you that I'm not forgotten but that You have a plan and a destiny for me this very day. Lord, please come into every situation in my home and bring Your peace and Your strength. Father, I thank You that through You, I can find purpose. As it says in Jeremiah 29:11, You have good plans for me, and if I look for You with my whole heart, I will find You. Today I search for You with my whole heart, and I ask You to come and meet me. I cling unto Your promises that offer me peace and hope for today and for my future! In Jesus' name. Amen.

Transformed by Love - Healing the Issues of the Heart
Day 14 – A Father to the Fatherless

Father to the fatherless, defender of widows—this is God, whose dwelling is holy.
Psalm 68:5 (NLT)

    As most of us probably know, there is One God, who is God, the Father, God, the Son, and God, the Holy Spirit. Today, I want to focus on God the Father. Some of us may have been abandoned and rejected by our earthly fathers. Perhaps your father was absent a lot, or maybe he was there but wasn't a very good father. This might have caused deep emotional wounds in your heart. Because we all need and desire a father's love, it can leave us wounded in diverse ways when that need isn't met. This vital relationship can affect the way we view our Heavenly Father. And it affects our belief system about ourselves and how we deserve to be treated. It can affect the relationship or lack thereof with our Heavenly Father. It affects our ability to have a connection with our Father God. For many of us, not dealing with or acknowledging this wound can lead to a distorted view of ourselves, causing us to internalize this rejection, abandonment, and hurt. We may feel that we are unworthy or unlovable, and it manifests through the relationships in our lives.
    Personally, I had a distorted view of Father God. I saw Him always being angry, distant, mad, hard to please, hard to understand, disappointed with me, cold, and unloving - just as my earthly dad was. I never had a healthy relationship with my father. Addiction and other factors in my childhood and throughout my life caused me to carry a lot of hurt in my heart toward my father for many years. At times, he was a cruel man. It caused me to have abandonment and rejection issues because of the strained relationship between my father and me. In addition, because of the many hurtful things he would call me, I had to really allow God to speak better words into my life. I didn't fully understand how influential a relationship between

Transformed by Love - Healing the Issues of the Heart
Day 14 – A Father to the Fatherless

> Father to the fatherless, defender of widows—this is God, whose dwelling is holy.
> Psalm 68:5 (NLT))

a daughter and a father could be. I've had many failed relationships, and I felt like every man who ever came into my life seemed to bring more hurt, abuse, and pain. I believed the lie that this was the way I deserved to be treated by men. I went out of my way to earn their love and continually gave of myself, but I always felt that I was never enough.

I grieved over never having a healthy relationship with my dad for many years. It wasn't until I really understood the heart of Father God that I was able to see myself as valuable and heal from my past. I understood my dad's pain and why he treated me the way he did. I invited Jesus into my wounds, into the memories of my childhood that caused me to feel this way about my father. I allowed the Lord to speak truth and love into my life and heal my wounds. I was able to forgive my dad for the past. I could love freely, without restraint, and without any expectations in return. I forgave my dad and the other men in my life that didn't treat me the way I deserved to be treated. My heavenly Father has been the most incredible Father I could ever ask for, loving me unconditionally, even in the lowest, darkest times in my life. That's the kind of love He offers us today. We can ask Him for a deeper revelation of His love, and He will be faithful to show us. I want you to invite Jesus into your 'father' wounds and allow Him to speak truth into the lies that have been ingrained into you. He desires to show you who He really is as a Father. Allow Father God to show you how to be loved as His child, and He will be faithful to show up in many ways.

Transformed by Love - Healing the Issues of the Heart
Day 14 – A Father to the Fatherless

> Father to the fatherless, defender of widows—this is God, whose dwelling is holy.
> Psalm 68:5 (NLT)

Your thoughts...

Prayer for Healing from Rejection and Abandonment

Father, I ask You to heal me from the issues of rejection and abandonment in my heart that may have been rooted there because of Fatherlessness. Lord, now that I know how important a relationship with a Father is in my life, I pray You would show me what a real Father should be like. Show me a deeper revelation of Your love for me as Your daughter. I acknowledge the pain I have in my heart because of this hurt. Heal these areas of my heart so that they won't manifest through the other personal relationships in my life. I pray that You would show me if I may have given myself too much in relationships to try and earn love. And heal the grief I have over never having a healthy relationship with my father. Show me Your heart, Father, that I would see myself as valuable in the same way You do. I forgive my earthly father for abandoning and rejecting me. I pray that You would speak truth and love into my life and heal my wounds. Thank You for Your truth and love, which bring me healing. In Jesus' name, I pray. Amen.

Transformed by Love - Healing the Issues of the Heart
Day 15 – Choose To Be Better Instead of Bitter

> Don't call me Naomi," she responded. "Instead, call me Mara, for the Almighty has made life very bitter for me. I went away full, but the Lord has bought me home empty. Why call me Naomi when the Lord has caused me to suffer and the Almighty has sent such tragedy upon me?
>
> Ruth 1:20, 21 (NLT)

The Bible story in the book of Ruth is about a mother named Naomi, who lived in the foreign country of Moab with her husband, Elimelech. They had two sons who eventually married Moabite women. Her two sons died, and she decided to return to her homeland. The famine, which had initially driven her and her husband out of Judah, was no longer an issue. Naomi released her two daughters-in-law, Ruth and Orpah, to stay in Moab with their families and try to remarry while she returned to her homeland. Ruth refused to leave Naomi and began the journey back with her to Judah. Although we tend to focus on how Ruth met Boaz, I want to focus a little bit on Naomi.

Twice in Ruth chapter 1, Naomi had blamed the Lord for her suffering. First, in 1:13(b), she states, "Things are far more bitter for me than you, because the Lord himself has raised his fist against me." The second time was in chapter 1, verse 20 (parentheses mine), where she says, "Don't call me Naomi... Instead, call me Mara (which means bitter) because the Almighty has made life very bitter for me. I went away full, but the LORD has bought me home empty. Why call me Naomi (which means pleasant one) when the LORD has caused me to suffer and the Almighty has sent such tragedy upon me?" Naomi's very name meant the opposite of bitter. But because she felt very bitter about her circumstances, she insisted they call her "Mara." Naomi blamed her unfortunate circumstances on the Lord. She claimed that He had caused her to suffer, which led to her bitterness toward Him

Bitterness can result from an emotional wound. The fruits of bitterness are anger, rage, aggression, resentment, jealousy, and misery, which cause you to observe those around you

Transformed by Love - Healing the Issues of the Heart
Day 15 – Choose To Be Better Instead of Bitter

> Don't call me Naomi," she responded. "Instead, call me Mara, for the Almighty has made life very bitter for me. I went away full, but the Lord has brought me home empty. Why call me Naomi when the Lord has caused me to suffer and the Almighty has sent such tragedy upon me?
>
> Ruth 1:20, 21 (NLT)

critically. Bitterness is so toxic that it can poison every relationship in your life if you hang on to it and allow it to fester. It will cause you to struggle to maintain relationships because you are easily wounded and have a negatively distorted view of the world. Bitter people have a hard time being positive. They criticize what others say and do. Bitterness robs people of joy. They are locked into the past or into those moments that caused them to be bitter, and they cannot find joy in the present.

When injustice, betrayal, hurt, pain, loss, or tragedy come our way, we must choose what we will do with that pain. We need to understand that we live in a fallen world and that pain will happen, but it is up to us how we will deal with it. We can either hold onto the pain that will make us bitter or give it to God and allow Him to deal with us and our situations to make us better. I had to give every hurt over to God - every wrong attitude, every person who mistreated me, whether intentionally or unintentionally. I chose to forgive because I could feel bitterness poisoning my heart. I made the decision to let go, and God began to bless my life. Naomi's life was eventually blessed again. Ruth was married and had a son with Boaz, which Naomi took as her own. When she let go of the bitterness, she could receive the blessings of God once again.

Transformed by Love - Healing the Issues of the Heart
Day 15 - Choose To Be Better Instead of Bitter

> Don't call me Naomi," she responded. "Instead, call me Mara, for the Almighty has made life very bitter for me. I went away full, but the Lord has bought me home empty. Why call me Naomi when the Lord has caused me to suffer and the Almighty has sent such tragedy upon me?
>
> Ruth 1:20, 21 (NLT)

Your thoughts...

Prayer Against Bitterness

Lord, I pray that You would help me let go of all bitterness in my heart. Father, heal this emotional wound in my heart that has caused the bitter fruits of anger, rage, aggression, resentment, and misery. Father, forgive me for allowing bitterness to poison every relationship in my life. I pray that You would heal the relationships in my life as You heal my heart. Please help me to allow situations to make me better instead of bitter. I speak joy and peace over my heart in areas where I can't find joy. I pray for the areas of my life where I have experienced betrayal, abuse, hurt, loss, and tragedy - all the areas of pain in my heart. Father, I ask that You bring healing and help me deal with this pain without it making me bitter. Lord, I hand my heart over to You. I hand every wrong attitude over to You. I give you every person who has mistreated me to You, and I decide to forgive today. I choose to let go so that You can bless my life once again. Amen.

Transformed by Love - Healing the Issues of the Heart
Day 16 – Don't Compare Your Pain

> The Lord is close to the broken-hearted; he rescues those whose spirits are crushed.
> Psalm 34:18 (NLT)

As I sat and watched a movie with a friend, she made a comment that got me thinking. The movie was about black slavery in America. The friend I was watching the show with said, "Wow, they really had it tough, didn't they? Way worse than we (Indigenous people) did." I replied, "I don't think you can compare pain & suffering - pain is pain. Although we experienced it in different ways, none is less than the other." I began to think deeper about this truth. Comparison causes us to minimize the effects of pain in our own hearts. Sometimes we go through hard things and don't acknowledge our pain because we always tell ourselves, "It could be worse" or "This person had it tougher, so I have no right to feel pain." When we don't validate our pain and suffering, we leave it unaddressed, and it will manifest in our lives in other ways. The pain must be validated and dealt with somehow. If not, it will show up in different ways, such as wrong thinking toward ourselves and others, or destructive cycles or patterns that we haven't been able to break. We may find ourselves triggered and overreacting in certain situations and not really understanding why.

Don't miss out on the healing Jesus wants to bring to your life by dismissing your pain. I believe that we will go through things that remind us that the pain is there. It will surface, and that is the Lord exposing it and wanting us to deal with it. Pain needs to be validated, confronted, and then healed with the truth of who God is. It's important to remember He has promises of healing and wholeness for us, and we can't recover from wounds we don't acknowledge are there.

It is also important to remember not to make pain an idol in

Transformed by Love – Healing the Issues of the Heart
Day 16 – Don't Compare Your Pain

The Lord is close to the broken-hearted; he rescues those whose spirits are crushed.
Psalm 34:18 (NLT)

our lives. It becomes an idol when we dwell on the pain and stay there, making no progress toward healing but always feeling victimized. Pain must be acknowledged, addressed, and dealt with, and then we move on until God shows us something else or takes us deeper into the same issue. When pain surfaces in our lives, we can go to God – acknowledge that pain, ask Him to show us how to deal with it, and speak His truth into those things.

Psalm 34:18 affirms that you are not alone! If you find yourself broken-hearted and crushed in spirit, know that God is with you! David, who wrote this Psalm, experienced all kinds of pain. He lost a child, and experienced terrible betrayal from a son and others. Yet, he always ran to the Lord for strength and comfort, which is why he is known as "a man after God's own heart." God's heart is for you. Run to Him with your pain and your troubles, and He will rescue you. He will not remove the memories of the pain, but He will heal your heart so that it doesn't affect you negatively anymore. You can be free from the effects of your pain and suffering. Go to God with your pain and be set free.

Transformed by Love - Healing the Issues of the Heart
Day 16 - Don't Compare Your Pain

The Lord is close to the broken-hearted; he rescues those whose spirits are crushed.
Psalm 34:18 (NLT)

Your thoughts...

Prayer for Dealing with Pain

Lord Jesus, I acknowledge the pain and the trauma that I have been through. Forgive me for comparing my pain to that of others and then pushing it down unresolved. I give the pain to You today, Lord, and I break off all destructive patterns and cycles created by not dealing with it. I invite You to bring healing into the areas of my life where it's needed. Thank You for exposing my pain so that I can deal with it. I pray that the truth of Your Word will bring healing to my heart. Thank You that I am not alone in my pain but that You are near the broken-hearted and the crushed in spirit. And just like You comforted and strengthened King David in Psalm 48, You will comfort and bring strength to me. You will heal my pain so that it doesn't affect me negatively anymore. In Jesus' name. Amen.

Transformed by Love – Healing the Issues of the Heart
Day 17 – The Rare Jewel of Contentment

> I know how to live on almost nothing or with everything. I have learned the secret of living in every situation, whether it is with a full stomach or empty, with plenty or little. For I can do everything through Christ, who gives me strength.
>
> Philippians 4:12, 13 (NLT)

Contentment is being blissfully satisfied and at peace with your circumstances, finding yourself in a place of completeness or wholeness, not in a position of need or unrest. The Apostle Paul wrote the above Scripture – he found true contentment in Christ. If you read the book of Acts, it is filled with the sufferings and persecutions of Paul. He was beaten, left for dead, stoned, imprisoned, and shipwrecked. He was in the most uncomfortable situations, yet he never gave up his vision and passion – preaching the gospel to the Jews and Gentiles. As long as he did this, he was satisfied no matter the conditions. This is the kind of godly contentment we must learn to abide in. Sometimes we may find ourselves fighting to stay content.

People worldwide are chasing the latest trends and technology. We may even be chasing after material possessions in hopes of filling a void in our lives. Our mindset might say, "If I can just have this, then I'll be happier," and when we get it, the joy is short-lived. The next trendy thing will come along and cost us so much to purchase, and in the next moment, we won't want it anymore.

I used to think external things could bring me contentment. I thought, "Oh, if I could just get my degree, then I'll be happy," or "If I could just get this great job, then I'll be happy," or "If I could just make good money, or travel more," and on and on it goes. And guess what? I obtained all these things and still felt a huge void in my life. I still felt empty at the end of the day. My relationship with God was shallow. I only prayed when I was in trouble or needed things. I continuously asked God to bless me with material wealth and possessions in my prayers, asking Him

Transformed by Love - Healing the Issues of the Heart
Day 17 – The Rare Jewel of Contentment

> I know how to live on almost nothing or with everything. I have learned the secret of living in every situation, whether it is with a full stomach or empty, with plenty or little. For I can do everything through Christ, who gives me strength.
>
> Philippians 4:12, 13 (NLT)

for what really mattered. At the end of the day, I was still very discontented, complaining, dissatisfied, and wanting more. It was never enough!

When I think back on this, I believe God gave me everything I asked for because He wanted to show me how it would never satisfy me. In reality, those possessions meant nothing. They perished, rusted, and broke. The rush I felt with each new thing always faded, and I became restless again. I learned to use my contentment to gauge my walk with God. If I overly desire something to the point of obsessing about it, I know that my relationship with God is lacking. Real godly contentment is attractive. It will attract the world because they will see that you are satisfied and at peace in your circumstances, even if they are not the best, according to the world's standards.

Godly contentment is a rare jewel, even among the body of Christ. We must always keep our hearts in check. Are we allowing the chase of something or someone to be more important than the chase of God? I know that God wants to bless us, even with material things. He never wants us to lack anything, but our priorities have to line up. We must discover this "secret" Paul talks about – learning to be content in every situation.

Transformed by Love - Healing the Issues of the Heart

Day 17 – The Rare Jewel of Contentment

I know how to live on almost nothing or with everything. I have learned the secret of living in every situation, whether it is with a full stomach or empty, with plenty or little. For I can do everything through Christ, who gives me strength.

Philippians 4:12, 13 (NLT)

Your thoughts...

Prayer for Contentment

Father, I thank you for stripping down the identity that I have unknowingly built for myself. Lord, forgive me for identifying with the things of this world. As I surrender my life to You, I pray that You would build me up into who You say I am. I pray that I will yield to every direction that You are leading me in, and I will trust You with every decision You make for my life. Thank You that I do not have to build my identity on the expectations of others or this world. Build me up in who You are and help me to accept Your love. Help me know that I am chosen, and I am a daughter of God, redeemed and sealed by Your Holy Spirit. Thank You for changing my life so that I am no longer pulled to please the world by titles and other people's expectations, but I am pulled to please You, my Heavenly Father. Amen.

Transformed by Love – Healing the Issues of the Heart

Day 18 – The Hidden Things of the Heart

> God, I invite your searching gaze into my heart. Examine me through and through; find out everything that may be hidden within me. Put me to the test and sift through all my anxious cares. See if there is any path of pain I'm walking on, and lead me back to your glorious, everlasting way— the path that brings me back to you.
>
> Psalm 139:23-24 (TPT)

God is so good. He is so gentle, so faithful, and so loving. He doesn't want us to stay the same, but to grow, flourish, and transform into His likeness. He wants us to experience freedom and peace, walk in His love, and know His heart. God's love lifts you up. It won't let you stay the same, but it will challenge you to address the areas in your life that may be contrary to God's truth. He will cause you to face what may be holding you back because He wants you to experience abundant life as His child.

I know I have hidden junk in my heart because the Lord continually shows me in His timing. One day while cleaning my basement, I turned the light on and started looking around. I thought to myself, "Wow, I didn't even know all this junk was down here until I turned on this light." The next moment, the Holy Spirit said something like this to me, "That's how your heart is. You don't realize the junk in there until I shed My light on those hidden things." Cleaning up junk is work. It's hard to look at the reality of all the junk you have stored in the basement of your heart - things that you didn't know were there.

I noticed that the Holy Spirit has used different ways of showing me the hidden things in my heart and when He does, I know that He's telling me, "It's time to address this." We could call this the "testing of the heart." One of the ways the Lord shows me is by allowing me to walk through uncomfortable situations that cause the ugly things in my heart to surface. One particular time, He brought someone into my life who was more gifted than I was, and it caused jealousy and envy to rise in me. If they hadn't been in my life for that season, I wouldn't have known

Transformed by Love - Healing the Issues of the Heart
Day 18 – The Hidden Things of the Heart

> God, I invite your searching gaze into my heart. Examine me through and through; find out everything that may be hidden within me. Put me to the test and sift through all my anxious cares. See if there is any path of pain I'm walking on, and lead me back to your glorious, everlasting way— the path that brings me back to you.
>
> Psalm 139:23-24 (TPT)

those sins were in my heart. The Lord has also used relationships in the church - both great and not-so-great - to build me up and show me what is in my heart. That's why being a part of a church family is so important. Just like in your natural family, growing up with your brothers and sisters, you may not have always gotten along with them. It is the same in the body of Christ with our spiritual brothers and sister. Sometimes they may rub us the wrong way, but instead of placing the finger of blame on them, ask God to reveal what is in your heart. He will be sure to show you.

Be vulnerable, honest, and open with God and allow Him to search your heart to expose and shed light on hidden things that are not pleasing to Him. He wants to help you overcome in these areas. As is stated in the above Scripture, let the Lord show you if there is any path of pain you may be walking on, and He will lead you back to His life-giving way.

Transformed by Love – Healing the Issues of the Heart
Day 18 – The Hidden Things of the Heart

> God, I invite your searching gaze into my heart. Examine me through and through; find out everything that may be hidden within me. Put me to the test and sift through all my anxious cares. See if there is any path of pain I'm walking on, and lead me back to your glorious, everlasting way— the path that brings me back to you.
>
> Psalm 139:23-24 (TPT)

Your thoughts...

Prayer for Exposing the Hidden Things in the Heart

Father, thank You for your love, which will never let me stay the same but will help me grow, flourish, and transform into Your likeness. Help me walk in such a way that I can experience freedom and peace and know Your heart. Thank You, Father, that Your love lifts me up. It challenges me to address the areas of my life that are contrary to who You are. Help me to face all that may be holding me back so that I can experience abundant life as Your child. Thank you for testing my heart and allowing me to walk through these situations that cause the junk in my heart to surface, as it's time to address it. Remove all envy, strife, and jealousy so that I can walk in love toward my brothers and sisters. Thank You that I can be vulnerable towards You. Help me be open and honest about my heart, allowing You to search it and shed light on the things hidden in there that are not pleasing to You. In Jesus' name. Amen.

Transformed by Love – Healing the Issues of the Heart
Day 19 – Great Worth in God's Sight

> Your beauty should not come from outward adornment, such as elaborated hairstyles and the wearing of gold jewelry or fine clothes. Rather, it should be that of your inner self, the unfading beauty of a gentle and quiet spirit, which is of great worth in God's sight.
>
> 1 Peter 3:3, 4 (NIV)

    I was crippled by insecurities in my younger days. I remember feeling very insecure, full of shame, and so self-conscious about the way I looked. I would rather opt out of opportunities than have any attention focused on me. I missed out on so much because I felt so ugly. I didn't realize that the critical way I felt about myself had filled me with self-hatred. Sometimes the voices inside our heads can be so loud, always screaming at us every time we look in the mirror, and pointing out our imperfections. They always magnify the imperfections of our bodies, so much so that it's all we can see, and we come to believe we will never be enough. These voices may have developed from a lack of positive affirmations, and support from our parents, social media, and the beauty industry that is always encouraging us to buy their products to "become" more beautiful. Not long ago, plastic surgery was rarely used by anyone other than aging Hollywood actors; nowadays, it is widespread, even among teenagers. If they don't like something about themselves, they can change it. I have worked with so many young girls who are crippled by insecurity to the point where they have so much self-hatred that they resort to self-harm, such as cutting. The unrealistic standards of manufactured beauty in this world are so damaging for our girls and women. As women of God, we are not to measure ourselves with this scale of beauty as the world does, but we are to seek the inner beauty of God in our lives.

    The world is so caught up with the outer appearance, but God looks at the heart - the inner beauty of a person - that is what has value. Our beauty is not an outward trait but one that is transformed into the likeness of Christ. The more that we

Transformed by Love - Healing the Issues of the Heart
Day 19 - Great Worth in God's Sight

> Your beauty should not come from outward adornment, such as elaborated hairstyles and the wearing of gold jewelry or fine clothes. Rather, it should be that of your inner self, the unfading beauty of a gentle and quiet spirit, which is of great worth in God's sight.
>
> 1 Peter 3:3, 4 (NIV)

become like Him, the more our inner beauty will overflow with the unfading beauty of God. We can be free from the world's unrealistic expectations of beauty. As I grew older, I stopped caring what other people might think about the way I looked and started learning to love myself. As I started to learn truths about the love of God, and how valuable I am to the Lord, I began to see myself as valuable. As I changed myself on the inside, I believe I became more beautiful on the outside because I was able to carry myself with confidence, no longer needing to measure my worth by the world's standards.

David was chosen to be the King of Israel because of his heart, not because of his looks. He is known as the greatest king Israel has ever had. In fact, when the Prophet Samuel first went to anoint a king, David was overlooked because of his appearance. In 1 Samuel 16:7b (NLT), the Lord said to Samuel regarding David, "The Lord doesn't see things the way you see them. People judge by outward appearance, but the Lord looks at the heart." And also, in Acts 13:22b (NLT) it states, "I have found David son of Jesse, a man after my own heart. He will do everything I want him to do." Isn't that beautiful? Even if you feel that you have been overlooked by people because of your appearance, you don't have to worry about being overlooked by God. He can do great things in your life if you seek His inner beauty. David is still well known today because of the heart he had after God He was so confident in who God was that He slayed a Philistine giant that an entire army refused to go against. This is the kind of destiny that God has for those of us who pursue His heart, those who pursue the inner beauty of the Lord.

Transformed by Love - Healing the Issues of the Heart
Day 19 - Great Worth in God's Sight

> Your beauty should not come from outward adornment, such as elaborated hairstyles and the wearing of gold jewelry or fine clothes. Rather, it should be that of your inner self, the unfading beauty of a gentle and quiet spirit, which is of great worth in God's sight.
>
> 1 Peter 3:3, 4 (NIV)

Your thoughts...

Prayer for Knowing my Worth

Father, I thank You for healing me from my insecurities and my self-hatred. Lord, help me to overcome these things that have held me back for so long. I pray that You would quiet the voices that speak louder than Your voice. Silence the voice of the enemy that comes to shout out all of my imperfections. Father, help me to work on what you consider beautiful – my inner self. Help me to focus on what you consider the true value of beauty. Father, I thank you that I am free from the world's unrealistic expectations of beauty and that I will embrace myself just as I am. Father, I thank you that my worth is not measured by the world's standards anymore, but my worth is measured on who You have created me to be. I pray that You would work inside me so that I can have the unfading beauty of a gentle and quiet spirit which is great worth to you. Amen.

Transformed by Love - Healing the Issues of the Heart
Day 20 – A Personal God

And I will ask the Father, and he will give you another Advocate, who will never leave you. He is the Holy Spirit, who leads into all truth. The world cannot receive him, because it isn't looking for him and doesn't recognize him. But you know him, because he lives with you now and later will be in you. No, I will not abandon you as orphans—I will come to you.

John 14:16-18 (NLT)

After Jesus' resurrection, He left to be seated at the right hand of God, but He promised to send us His Holy Spirit, which He did. Now we have the Holy Spirit living within us. You can't get more intimate than that. God will never leave us to deal with the issues in our hearts by ourselves. We have the Spirit of the Living God inside us who will lead us into truth. He is our Comforter, our Counsellor, and someone who comes alongside us in our struggles. He corrects us, leads us, and guides us. He promises to walk with us day-by-day, so we will never be abandoned. We can walk in intimacy with the Holy Spirit. The word intimacy simply means to walk in closeness. Because of its obsession with sex, the world has twisted its meaning. True intimacy with God is a place of closeness, trust, and vulnerability with Him. It is trusting Him because He knows every detail of our life, even the darkness, and He still loves us unconditionally. No one, not even the closest people in our lives, know us as Jesus knows us. Since the beginning of time, the Lord has been there, and He knows everything you have walked through. Jesus remembers when you were born and every detail of your life that you are not even capable of remembering. He knows the number of hairs on your head, which cannot be counted. Psalm 139 says His thoughts for us are more than the grains of sand. Can you imagine that? When we pick up a handful of sand on a beach, we cannot count every grain of sand in our hands, yet the Lord's thoughts of us are greater than that.

When you are intimate with someone, you can trust them, sharing things you wouldn't necessarily tell just anyone. There may have been a time when others have broken your trust, but

Transformed by Love - Healing the Issues of the Heart
Day 20 – A Personal God

> And I will ask the Father, and he will give you another Advocate, who will never leave you. He is the Holy Spirit, who leads into all truth. The world cannot receive him, because it isn't looking for him and doesn't recognize him. But you know him, because he lives with you now and later will be in you. No, I will not abandon you as orphans—I will come to you.
>
> John 14:16-18 (NLT)

you can trust the Lord. It may hurt to bring painful situations up again but the path to intimacy is to give them to Jesus. If you want the closest of relationships with God, you need to risk opening your heart. There's no other way. It has been during the most challenging times in my life that Jesus has shown Himself the most real. I thank the Lord for trials and hardships because I experience His love in ways I never have before. I was able to experience Him as a Comforter during loss, a Counsellor during confusing times, and a Guide when the path I had to walk down was dark. This is the kind of intimacy we have available with Jesus. When you have Jesus, you are no longer alone. This isn't just a thought; it's a reality. You can experience being led by His Spirit and hearing His voice. You can invite Him into the places where you have fear or shame, and He will speak truth into your heart.

God is with you, and He is for you. He longs to spend time with you, heal you, and share the secrets of His heart with you. He desires to show you the good things He has for you. Trust in Him with all your heart.

Transformed by Love – Healing the Issues of the Heart
Day 20 – A Personal God

> And I will ask the Father, and he will give you another Advocate, who will never leave you. He is the Holy Spirit, who leads into all truth. The world cannot receive him, because it isn't looking for him and doesn't recognize him. But you know him, because he lives with you now and later will be in you. No, I will not abandon you as orphans—I will come to you.
>
> John 14:16-18 (NLT)

Your thoughts...

Prayer to Embrace the Holy Spirit

Father, I thank You for Your Holy Spirit that lives inside me. Holy Spirit, thank You for the intimacy that You offer. You never leave me to deal with the issues of my heart by myself, but You, Holy Spirit, will lead me into all truth. You are my Comforter, my Counsellor, and someone who comes alongside me in my struggles. You lead me, guide me, and never abandon me. You walk with me day by day in intimacy with You. Thank You that I can trust You and be vulnerable with You because You know every detail of my life. Even in my sin, You still love me unconditionally. Father, thank You that You know every detail of my life, yet You still love me. I can trust You with sharing the intimate things of my heart. I pray that I could have true, deep intimacy with You, Jesus, and I can experience being led by Your spirit and hearing Your voice. I invite You into those areas. Thank You for healing my heart, being there for me, and showing me the secrets of Your heart. Thank You that You have great things in store for me when I give my heart to You and trust You with my whole heart. In Jesus' name, I pray. Amen.

Transformed by Love – Healing the Issues of the Heart
Day 21 – Facing Your Shame

> Then Jesus stood up again and said to the woman, "Where are your accusers? Didn't even one of them condemn you?" "No, Lord," she said. And Jesus said, "Neither do I. Go and sin no more."
>
> John 8: 10, 11 (NLT)

In John chapter 8, there is a story about a woman caught in adultery. The teachers of the religious law brought her before Jesus and the crowd, exposing her sin of adultery in front of them. Because the crowd loved Jesus and He had a reputation for showing mercy, they hoped He would condemn the woman and lose favour with the crowd. They wanted Jesus to judge her and agree to stone her to death, which was justified under the law of Moses. Instead, Jesus did something profound. He said, "Whoever has no sin, throw the first stone." One by one, her accusers all walked away, and Jesus told the woman, "Go and sin no more." The religious leaders used the woman caught in adultery as a pawn to trap Jesus without considering her feelings and humiliating her. Can you imagine the shame and embarrassment she must have felt? Getting caught in adultery, which was considered immoral, dishonourable, and improper, was punishable by death under the law. In addition to this, her sin was exposed before Jesus and the entire town. She was probably expecting to be stoned to death. Yet, Jesus showed such compassion in His dealings with her. He worked things out on her behalf, giving her a second chance. Jesus is the God of second chances. He has so much patience with us, helping us overcome our sin and shame. Jesus' response taught us a lot about His loving nature. Because of His love, compassion, and gentleness, her life was spared. Condemnation accuses. It says, "You are guilty!" It seeks punishment and passes judgment. Conviction points you to the cross and says, "You are forgiven; sin no more."

Sister, it's time to stop looking inward. It is time to stop looking at the shame of your past, and the dark days you lived apart

Transformed by Love - Healing the Issues of the Heart
Day 21 – Facing Your Shame

Then Jesus stood up again and said to the woman, "Where are your accusers? Didn't even one of them condemn you?" "No, Lord," she said. And Jesus said, "Neither do I. Go and sin no more."

John 8: 10, 11 (NLT)

from God. No matter what kind of shame it is, Jesus looks at you with compassion and forgiveness, but you must also forgive yourself. When we look at ourselves with such harsh criticism, we can fail to see what God offers us today. He offers us His mercy and forgiveness. Shame can take root in our hearts in all kinds of ways. Personally, because I was a victim of sexual abuse as a child, I held onto shame for most of my life. I believed the lies of the enemy for the longest time. I was convinced that I did something to deserve being treated that way by those men. I thought there was something wrong with me, and somehow what happened to me as a child was my fault, and it caused me to carry a lot of shame. It wasn't until the love and mercy of Christ came in that I recognized my value in Him. We are powerless as children when things happen to us, but when we don't face our shame, it can cause us to do things that bring even more guilt. Open your heart to the mercy and compassion of Christ and know that John 3:17 says that Jesus came to save us, not condemn and judge us. Jesus does so much more than deliver us from our sin. He restores and heals all the pain that darkness has caused. Receive His forgiveness today and allow Him to remove the sting of shame just as He did with the woman caught in adultery.

Transformed by Love - Healing the Issues of the Heart
Day 21 – Facing Your Shame

> Then Jesus stood up again and said to the woman, "Where are your accusers? Didn't even one of them condemn you? "No, Lord," she said. And Jesus said, "Neither do I. Go and sin no more."
>
> John 8: 10, 11 (NLT)

Your thoughts...

Prayer to Release Shame

Father, show me where I may have hidden shame. And, in return, I give all of it over to You today. Help me to accept Your deep love, truth, and forgiveness where I may have been hanging onto shame. Remove the blinders of guilt and restore my integrity and honour. Help me continue walking free of shame every day as I walk with You. In Jesus' name. Amen.

Transformed by Love – Healing the Issues of the Heart
Day 22 – He Will Meet You in Your Darkness

> Later, Matthew invited Jesus and his disciples to his home as dinner guests, along with many tax collectors and other disreputable sinners. But when the Pharisees saw this, they asked his disciples, "Why does your teacher eat with such scum?" When Jesus heard this, he said, "Healthy people don't need a doctor—sick people do." Then he added, "Now go and learn the meaning of this Scripture: 'I want you to show mercy, not offer sacrifices.' For I have come to call NOT those who think they are righteous, but those who know they are sinners."
>
> Matthew 9:10–13 (NLT)

Do you know that God still loves you even in the darkest, most shameful and sinful times of your life? Do you realize He is still longing to know you, and wants to meet you right now, right where you are? You don't have to "get clean" or "act right" before you come to God! You are never too lost or too far gone for Him. In fact, that is why God sent His only Son, Jesus, to die and set us free from the sin and darkness in our lives. Jesus came to take all that darkness on Himself so we wouldn't have to carry it. Jesus is saying to you, "Come as you are."

I remember the days when I was engulfed in my sin. I was addicted, depressed, feeling hopeless, and filled with so much shame. I would whisper to God, "One day, I will turn to You, Lord. When I stop sinning, I will come. When I'm a better person, I will come to You. Wait for me to overcome this addiction, and then I'll go to church." I didn't know that I could come to Him just as I was, and He would deliver me from the addiction and burden of my sin! I had this assumption that I was too dirty, too lost, and too much in darkness to go to Him. I figured the Lord looked at me the same way people treated me - with judgment and impatience. But now I know the truth, and I'm telling you that He can and will meet you right where you are at. You don't have to try in your own strength to be better. Jesus will help you get better - way better! Through His Holy Spirit that fills and empowers us, we become better, healed, and full of the love of God.

The Gospels are filled with stories of Jesus hanging out with those whom the religious leaders considered the worst type of

Transformed by Love – Healing the Issues of the Heart
Day 22 – He Will Meet You in Your Darkness

> Later, Matthew invited Jesus and his disciples to his home as dinner guests, along with many tax collectors and other disreputable sinners. But when the Pharisees saw this, they asked his disciples, "Why does your teacher eat with such scum?" When Jesus heard this, he said, "Healthy people don't need a doctor—sick people do." Then he added, "Now go and learn the meaning of this Scripture: 'I want you to show mercy, not offer sacrifices.' For I have come to call NOT those who think they are righteous, but those who know they are sinners."
>
> Matthew 9:10–13 (NLT)

sinners. Jesus met them exactly where they were! He didn't say, "Get away from me and come back when you start acting properly!" No, He extended His grace to them, accepted them, and ate with them (which, in that day, was considered an intimate gesture). Before they repented, changed anything, or started following Him, Jesus took the time to show them that He cared.

Jesus came to die for our sins. He died a criminal's death even though He was innocent and didn't deserve it. He did it willingly for all of us. He carried our sin and shame so we wouldn't have to. The world has a measuring stick that categorizes one sin as worse than another, but Jesus came to die for all the sins of the world. Be encouraged that we can meet Jesus as we are. He will help us to change by empowering us with His Spirit. We don't have to try to get right on our own first; Jesus will come and dine with you, accept you, and love you just as you are. He will give you the strength and desire to change. You don't have to do it on your own. Invite Him into your darkness, and He will gladly come and dine with you.

Transformed by Love - Healing the Issues of the Heart
Day 22 – He Will Meet You in Your Darkness

> Later, Matthew invited Jesus and his disciples to his home as dinner guests, along with many tax collectors and other disreputable sinners. But when the Pharisees saw this, they asked his disciples, "Why does your teacher eat with such scum?" When Jesus heard this, he said, "Healthy people don't need a doctor—sick people do." Then he added, "Now go and learn the meaning of this Scripture: 'I want you to show mercy, not offer sacrifices.' For I have come to call NOT those who think they are righteous, but those who know they are sinners."
>
> Matthew 9:10–13 (NLT)

Your thoughts...

Prayer to Allow God into Your Darkness

Lord, I ask You to meet me right where I am today, in my darkness and sin. I know that I don't have the power to overcome sin on my own, so I ask for Your help today. I understand that my own righteousness is filthy rags, and that true righteousness comes from You. Come and shine Your light in the dark areas of my heart, and the places that I may not even realize I am withholding from You. Holy Spirit, fill me with Your presence. I accept Your love and completely surrender to You, God. In Jesus' name, I pray. Amen.

Transformed by Love – Healing the Issues of the Heart
Day 23 – My Prince of Peace

Don't let your hearts be troubled. Trust in God, and trust also in me..."I am leaving you with a gift—peace of mind and heart. And the peace I give is a gift the world cannot give. So don't be troubled or afraid."

John 14:1, 27 (NLT)

For many years I struggled with depression. I can't even tell you if there was a time when I wasn't depressed before I came to Christ, because it was all I knew. Depression is the overwhelming, continuous feeling of being sad. This sadness seems to overtake your life to the point where everything feels like such an effort. Your energy level is low, and you seem to lose interest and excitement in day-to-day life. It affects every area of your life, including how you think, feel, and act. It encompasses feelings of worthlessness and can affect your ability to concentrate. You may even have thoughts of harming yourself. Depression troubles the soul and mind. It does not let you experience peace but keeps you in constant darkness with an inability to feel joy.

I believe my depression stemmed from growing up in an environment of constant uncertainty. I come from an impoverished, alcoholic home and continuously witnessed domestic violence throughout my childhood. Then I personally struggled with addiction through my early teens and into adulthood. All of this contributed to my struggle with depression. In my mid-twenties, I began searching for peace. I lived in such torment in my mind and emotions that I couldn't rest. I tried all kinds of ways to find relief, but in the end, I never could. I was losing myself, digging into a deeper and deeper hole. I knew that if I continued self-medicating with alcohol, I would die, or completely lose myself. I was ready to find a way out of this downhill spiral I was in.

In John 14:1, Jesus was encouraging His disciples not to be troubled that He was going away, so He urged them to trust Him. The disciples had just finished spending three years being

Transformed by Love - Healing the Issues of the Heart
Day 23 – My Prince of Peace

> Don't let your hearts be troubled. Trust in God, and trust also in me…"I am leaving you with a gift—peace of mind and heart. And the peace I give is a gift the world cannot give. So don't be troubled or afraid."
>
> John 14:1, 27 (NLT)

taught by Jesus. Soon it would be time for Him to go to the cross and finish what He came to the world to accomplish - be crucified, die, and rise from the dead. Jesus' disciples loved Him so much they did not want to see Him leave. Regardless, it was something that Jesus had to do to complete His work and send the Holy Spirit to live in us. In verse 27, He made a promise to His disciples, which also applies to us this very day. Jesus promised them "peace of mind and heart," not as the world gives, but the kind that only comes from Him. This is His supernatural peace that works in every circumstance and situation we face.

Depression doesn't let us rest; we have so much inner turmoil that we cannot seem to have peace. I remember when I experienced His peace for the first time. I was sitting in church with my eyes closed in the presence of God. I felt this peace come over me, and I could feel the weight of depression lift. It was as though a stack of bricks had been taken off my shoulders. I felt light, my vision was clearer, and I experienced the peace I was looking for, and it has never left me. I dug deeper into peace as I've learned more about who God is. This peace doesn't come from this world, and it stays with me through both the good and dark times. It overtakes my mind and heart and creates strength in my life through trying times. It is only offered by the Prince of Peace, Jesus Christ. Allow God to be your peace and take the weight of depression off your life right now.

Transformed by Love - Healing the Issues of the Heart
Day 23 – My Prince of Peace

> Don't let your hearts be troubled. Trust in God, and trust also in me..."I am leaving you with a gift—peace of mind and heart. And the peace I give is a gift the world cannot give. So don't be troubled or afraid."
>
> John 14:1, 27 (NLT)

Your thoughts...

Prayer for Peace

Father, I ask You for Your peace that surpasses all circumstances and understanding. Let Your peace cover my heart and my mind today. Deliver me from depression and forgive me where I have allowed it to come in. Jesus, help me stay in Your peace by staying close to You. Forgive me for allowing thoughts into my mind that caused me to feel hopeless and depressed. I ask You to give me a clear mind and new hope in You and fill me with Your joy. Help me to have the strength to reach out and ask for help if I need it. Thank You that I don't have to carry the burdens of life alone. Lord, I trust You and ask You to work in every circumstance in my life and bring peace through the good and the bad times. In Jesus' name, I pray. Amen.

Transformed by Love - Healing the Issues of the Heart
Day 24 - Fighting Anxiety

Trust in the Lord completely, and do not rely on your own opinions. With all your heart rely on him to guide you, and he will lead you in every decision that you make. Become intimate with him in whatever you do, and he will lead you wherever you go.

Proverbs 3:5, 6 (TPT)

I know the anxiety in my life developed from not trusting God and allowing negative thoughts to get the best of me. Often, I have found myself thinking excessively or obsessively about potential future problems or challenges that haven't yet taken place. When I allow the "what ifs" to speak louder than the truth and reality of who God is, I get anxious feelings that try to steal my peace.

In the past few years, I experienced several unpleasant things that tried to rock my foundation and caused me to develop anxious thoughts. I find myself still fighting anxious thoughts most days, but I'm aware of them and am learning to stand in peace in those areas.

The Covid pandemic brought so much fear and uncertainty with it. It plagued the nations of the world to the point where everything completely shut down. When I had Covid, the sickness was more an illness to my mind than it was to my body. I was one of the first to have Covid among my friends, family, church, and co-workers. With Covid came so much hype, fear, shame, and uncertainty, and this was what I fought through the entire time of having it. Rather than fighting the symptoms, I was fighting the turmoil in my mind and heart. While I was sick, I became obsessed with the surfaces I touched. I was scared that I had infected the people I hugged or hung out with before knowing I had Covid. I became so anxious because I knew that the things I was thinking could be a reality. I isolated alone in my bedroom for fourteen days, and didn't leave my home for three weeks, fighting these thoughts. I prayed and worshiped God, but the anxiety seemed to speak louder than His voice and I allowed it to get the best of me. The stigma of getting Covid

Transformed by Love - Healing the Issues of the Heart
Day 24 – Fighting Anxiety

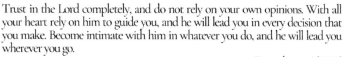

> Trust in the Lord completely, and do not rely on your own opinions. With all your heart rely on him to guide you, and he will lead you in every decision that you make. Become intimate with him in whatever you do, and he will lead you wherever you go.
>
> Proverbs 3:5, 6 (TPT)

appears to have lessened now, and it doesn't seem as big of a deal anymore, which is excellent! If you find yourself relating to my situation, you and I both know that it can be a battle.

When we go through things that cause us to feel anxious, we may be tempted to think God has forgotten or abandoned us. Anxiety causes you to believe thoughts that are not the truth. Expecting bad things to happen will steal your peace and joy. Instead of focusing on what is true, it causes you to focus on future "what ifs" - things that haven't even happened. We need to quiet those voices when they speak. Anxiety does not trust God but puts trust in potentially negative situations. When things happen that feel like they rock our foundation, we should consider God's truths for us. We need to trust in the Lord and not our own opinions, or for that matter, the world's opinions. We need to remain in intimacy with Him and allow His Words to be the focus of our lives.

Transformed by Love - Healing the Issues of the Heart
Day 24 - Fighting Anxiety

Trust in the Lord completely, and do not rely on your own opinions. With all your heart rely on him to guide you, and he will lead you in every decision that you make. Become intimate with him in whatever you do, and he will lead you wherever you go.

Proverbs 3:5, 6 (TPT)

Prayer Against Anxiety

Father, forgive me for not trusting You and allowing anxious thoughts to enter my mind. I will not allow the enemy to speak louder than Your voice. Heal me from my anxious thoughts and help me to be aware of thoughts that do not line up to Your Word. I declare Your peace over my life. Thank You, Lord, that I can trust You in every circumstance and that my future is secure in You. In Jesus' Name. Amen.

Transformed by Love - Healing the Issues of the Heart
Day 25 – Be Renewed Every Day

> That is why we never give up. Though our bodies are dying, our spirits are being renewed every day.
>
> 2 Corinthians 4:16 (NLT)

When we are born again, we become a new creation – our spirits are immediately made right with God; they are instantly made brand new. Our souls (emotions, mind, and will) need to be renewed and transformed by the Word and the reality of God. Some things happen immediately, while others take time. It is a gradual change. We need to continually seek the truth of the Word, walk in it, and stay in a relationship with Jesus for our hearts and lives to change. We live in a fallen world, and life will always be far from perfect. We will suffer loss, rejection, and all kinds of hurts that we need God to heal. We will also go through times of blessing and abundance, seasons that we will love and not want to end, but in comfortable times we grow the least. We all must go through the process of transformation without giving up. Healing from past wounds is a part of that. It is a necessary component of the transitioning process. Wounds cause our view to be distorted, so the right mindset and heart change are essential if we want to experience God's true blessings.

We experience different seasons naturally, and as much as we may prefer one over the other, they must come to an end. Spiritually, it is the same. Seasons of new growth (spring), seasons of enjoying the abundance and fruitfulness of the land (summer), seasons of harvest and pruning (fall), and seasons of death (winter), where only the deep roots survive and the cold kills everything on the surface. If we allow them, these periods of time will eventually work out for good, building character and showing us who God is in our lives. Even if they are challenging and uncomfortable, we must embrace them because each transition prepares us for the next. Preparation and transformation are necessary and will grow good fruit in our

Transformed by Love – Healing the Issues of the Heart
Day 25 – Be Renewed Every Day

> That is why we never give up. Though our bodies are dying, our spirits are being renewed every day.
>
> 2 Corinthians 4:16 (NLT)

lives. If we want to truly experience a new of level of freedom, we must submit and embrace each one as it comes so we can walk in all that God has for us. As each period passes, we are renewed into His image, and His character is being worked out in our lives.

As stated in the Scripture we used above, Paul, the author of Corinthians, knew about transitioning and the renewal process because he had been through it. Even his name was changed. He transitioned from Saul to Paul, from persecutor of Christians to preacher of the Gospel. Saul killed Christians until he had an encounter with Jesus that changed him forever. His dramatic change was evident throughout the New Testament as he sought to convert Jews and Gentiles. If Paul had to go through times of transition, so do we. We can embrace each season, trusting God that He will always remain the same even when our circumstances change. He will be the stability in our lives. God will be faithful to see us through each and every season that comes our way. As we submit to the transitioning and renewal process, we will begin to experience Jesus in different ways. The transition will be worth it!

Transformed by Love - Healing the Issues of the Heart
Day 25 – Be Renewed Every Day

That is why we never give up. Though our bodies are dying, our spirits are being renewed every day.

2 Corinthians 4:16 (NLT)

Your thoughts...

Prayer to be Renewed

Father, I thank You for the process of being renewed by Your Spirit day by day. Thank You that when I accepted You as my Saviour, You immediately gave me a new Spirit - Your Spirit, but it doesn't stop there. You continue to heal my soul every day. I pray that You will help me be patient with myself as Your Word and Your reality transform me. I trust You with the healing of my heart. Help me to stay in relationship with You while I heal. Let me walk through each season of life gracefully and wholeheartedly with You. As Paul said in 2 Corinthians 4:16, I say that I will never give up. I will continue the process of being renewed and submitting to what You are doing in my life in every season. In Jesus' name. Amen.

Transformed by Love - Healing the Issues of the Heart

Day 26 - Rejected by Man, Accepted by Christ

> He came to his own people, and even they rejected him. But to all who believed him and accepted him, he gave the right to become children of God.
> John 1:11,12 (NLT)

Rejection can be either real or perceived. Perceived rejection includes actions done toward you that can cause you to feel rejected, but it may not have been intentional. Perhaps you didn't receive an invitation to an important event that everyone else was invited to, or maybe someone didn't respond to a message even though they saw it, or they said no and shut down an idea you had. When these things cause a reaction in us, there is usually a deeper issue in our hearts - a root of rejection that could stem from various negative childhood experiences. Some causes include never being told you were loved by your parents, neglect – not having your basic needs met, feeling insecure or unprotected in your home, being left alone, or abandoned by your parents and raised by someone else. Either way, rejection hurts. Everyone has experienced it at some point in their lives. You may have had a romantic interest in someone who didn't feel the same way toward you. Maybe your significant other decided to end your relationship because they weren't interested in you anymore. Perhaps you were rejected by an organization that hired someone else for the position you wanted, or you didn't make the sports team you worked hard to join. Rejection can totally cripple a person to the point that they refuse to take risks because the sting is too much. Life is full of rejections, but we should be resilient enough to bounce back and sufficiently deal with it in a healthy manner and move forward.

You know you have a problem with rejection when you do everything in your power not to be rejected. You avoid situations that could leave you feeling that way. Rejection allows the opinions of others to determine who you are, and you become overly sensitive to their criticism. It causes you to be a

Transformed by Love - Healing the Issues of the Heart
Day 26 – Rejected by Man, Accepted by Christ

> He came to his own people, and even they rejected him. But to all who believed him and accepted him, he gave the right to become children of God.
>
> John 1:11,12 (NLT)

people-pleaser instead of a God-pleaser. You continually fight the thought that you are not wanted, and even doubt Jesus' love for you. It causes you to believe there is something wrong with you. It can cause you to keep people at a distance, never allowing them in, because if they find out who you really are, they may reject you.

Rejection is a strategy of Satan – we need to be in agreement with what Jesus says about us, not what Satan says. Jesus says that we are loved, accepted, and worthy. We can ask God for a deeper revelation of His love so that we don't just "say" we are loved, but we "know" we are loved. God always desires to come closer to us, and the love of Christ will cause us to know who we are in Him. We are His children, and He loves us fully. He will never try to get away from us. If you think about how much you love your own children, Jesus' love for you is even deeper. His love will give us the proper perspective about people and God. It will help us respond the right way in the face of rejection.

The way that Jesus dealt with rejection is the perfect example for us to learn from. The people in His hometown rejected Him. His own people, the Jews, rejected Him so much that they pushed for His crucifixion on the cross. The way they treated Him did not change who Jesus was or the direction that God was taking Him in. He continued to accomplish His God-given destiny to die for our sins, overcome death, and be resurrected. He trusted God, regardless of His feelings.

Transformed by Love - Healing the Issues of the Heart
Day 26 – Rejected by Man, Accepted by Christ

He came to his own people, and even they rejected him. But to all who believed him and accepted him, he gave the right to become children of God.
John 1:11,12 (NLT)

Your thoughts...

Prayer for Rejection

Lord, I ask you to pull out the roots of rejection that are in my heart and heal me from its effects. I pray that I will be aware of Satan's strategies, and I come into agreement with You that I am loved, accepted, and worthy. Give me a deeper revelation of Your love so that I know I am Yours, and I am accepted by You just as I am. Help me to always face rejection in a healthy way so that it no longer cripples me. I will not make decisions based on the fear of rejection. Thank You Lord for uprooting and healing this area of my heart. I will move forward into all that You have called me to walk in. In Jesus' name. Amen.

Transformed by Love – Healing the Issues of the Heart
Day 27 – Breaking off the Poverty Mindset

> Wealth and honour come from you alone, you rule over everything. Power and might are in your hand, and at your discretion people are made great and given strength...Everything we have has come from you, and we give you only what you first gave us!
>
> 1 Chronicles 29:12, 14b (NLT)

I grew up in poverty. During my entire childhood and early adult years, I was always lacking. And because of that, I never noticed certain mindsets I developed. A poverty mindset influences our behaviours and beliefs regarding how we deal with money. It conditioned me to believe that I would never have enough, and that is just how life was. A poverty mentality can cause you to have beliefs that include, you shouldn't spend money on non-essentials, feeling guilty when you have more than someone else, hoarding what you do have, feeling like you never have enough resources, always taking the cheaper alternative, never taking risks, being constantly worried about money, or disliking rich people.

In my case, I was taught to have little value for money because my family didn't have much of it, and what you don't value, you give no mind to.

When I finally started making money after graduating from university, I didn't know how to handle it, so I spent irresponsibly. In fact, I dug myself into debt because I couldn't manage all the money and credit that was accessible to me. I knew that I wasn't a good steward of what I had and that the Lord wanted more for me. I was so used to struggling to make ends meet that when I had enough, I didn't know how to handle it. I would sabotage my prosperity by making poor financial decisions. I know it sounds absurd, but I really did that. If things were going well, it made me uncomfortable.

The verses quoted above were written by King David. He praised God because all the needs were met to build a costly temple for the Lord. King David was extremely wealthy, as was his son, King Solomon, who took the throne after him, and they

Transformed by Love - Healing the Issues of the Heart
Day 27 – Breaking off the Poverty Mindset

> Wealth and honour come from you alone, you rule over everything. Power and might are in your hand, and at your discretion people are made great and given strength...Everything we have has come from you, and we give you only what you first gave us!
>
> 1 Chronicles 29:12, 14b (NLT)

both loved the Lord. Riches and wealth did not overtake them, for they knew that the means of this world were fleeting. They understood that everything they had was from God and that the riches were not theirs. We need to have this same mindset. We must understand that we can never outgive God. When we recognize that, it is easier to release it when He asks us to do so. We do not need to hold on in fear that we won't have enough.

How do we break off this poverty mindset? I can share with you some ways that have worked for me. I learned to be grateful for what He has given me, and I continue to thank the Lord for blessing me. I have become more generous and expanded my views about money. God wants me to be a good steward of what I have, so I am faithful in tithes and offerings. I've realized that it's okay to spoil myself within reason. Am I rich? No! But I've learned how to be a good steward of what I have, and in return, the Lord continues to bless me. We may not be rich monetarily, but we are people of influence, and we must carry ourselves as such. If we don't understand the value we have in the Kingdom, we will carry ourselves carelessly, saying and doing things without realizing the impact we have. Let's not love money or be ruled by it, but use it as a tool to bless and further the Kingdom of God!

Transformed by Love - Healing the Issues of the Heart
Day 27 – Breaking off the Poverty Mindset

Wealth and honour come from you alone, you rule over everything. Power and might are in your hand, and at your discretion people are made great and given strength...Everything we have has come from you, and we give you only what you first gave us!

1 Chronicles 29:12, 14b (NLT)

Your thoughts...

Prayer Against a Poverty Mindset

Thank you, Father, that all wealth and honour come from You. You alone have the power and might in Your hands. Thank You for changing my thinking and helping me accept all the blessings You have for me. Help me overcome this poverty mindset by teaching me new things about finances. I want to be a good steward of what I have. Help me to know that I am worthy of more. Help me understand the value of what I have been given, and to always be grateful for it. In Jesus' name. Amen.

Transformed by Love - Healing the Issues of the Heart
Day 28 - God will Never Abandon You

> We are pressed on every side by troubles, but we are not crushed. We are perplexed, but not driven to despair. We are hunted down, but never abandoned by God. We get knocked down, but we are not destroyed.
> 2 Corinthians 4:8, 9 (NLT)

When people you love walk away from you it can be devastating. I recognized that the root of my abandonment issues came when my mom and dad's relationship ended. My dad left my mom for another woman, and I never saw him for months after he left. Mom turned to alcohol to ease her pain, and I would go days without seeing her. My siblings and I were left to fend for ourselves through this time. It caused so much uncertainty, anxiety, and fear in my life, but most of all, it left a root of abandonment that I had to face as an adult. Like most children, I thought I was the cause of my parents break up. I remember so vividly feeling hurt and not understanding why neither of my parents were concerned with how we were affected by their choices. I felt unworthy and lonely for my parents and didn't understand why things were the way they were. It was such a devastating time for a ten-year-old, and my entire life crumbled. The security that I once felt from having my parents around was no longer there. It felt like we were left unprotected, unloved, uncared for, and completely abandoned. My oldest sister read to us from the Bible and even though I didn't understand, I remember the peace and comfort that came over me in those times. That season in my life was a long one; it continued into my teen years. I had way too much freedom as a pre-teen and teen and had to do deal with the consequences of those poor decisions when I grew up.

As an adult, issues of abandonment can cause you to feel insecure in your relationships. You may have difficulty trusting people and struggle to believe they will stay in your life. You won't allow people to be invested in any type of relationship with you. Abandonment ties in with rejection and low

Transformed by Love – Healing the Issues of the Heart
Day 28 – God will Never Abandon You

> We are pressed on every side by troubles, but we are not crushed. We are perplexed, but not driven to despair. We are hunted down, but never abandoned by God. We get knocked down, but we are not destroyed.
>
> 2 Corinthians 4:8, 9 (NLT)

self-esteem. It can cause you to try too hard to make the other person happy so they will stay, even if it costs you and leaves you feeling drained.

Jesus knew exactly how it felt to be abandoned when He was on the cross. He had to carry the sins of the world by Himself. His disciples had all scattered, and for that moment, while He had the weight of sin on His shoulders, God turned away, the sun grew dark, and Jesus cried out, "My God, my God, why have you abandoned me?" Matthew 27:46b (NLT). Jesus experienced the ultimate abandonment. Everyone had left him. He must have felt completely alone on the cross, enduring what He had to all alone. I am so grateful that He carried our abandonment issues so we wouldn't have to. Scripture is filled with promises where the Lord says He will never leave us. I know that He was with me throughout all that time when my parents abandoned me. And now that I know Him, I always feel Him so close; I never feel alone or abandoned. Even when I struggle as a single mom, I know He is there because He comforts me with His presence.

Transformed by Love – Healing the Issues of the Heart

Day 28 – God will Never Abandon You

> We are pressed on every side by troubles, but we are not crushed. We are perplexed, but not driven to despair. We are hunted down, but never abandoned by God. We get knocked down, but we are not destroyed.
>
> 2 Corinthians 4:8, 9 (NLT)

Your thoughts...

Prayer to Heal Abandonment Issues

Father, thank You that You paid the ultimate price for me, including my abandonment issues. Thank You, Jesus, for showing me that You knew what it was like to be abandoned when You faced the cross. Help me feel secure in my relationship with You and teach me to trust people again. Thank You for building me up and showing me who I am in You. I am loved and accepted by You, and You will never leave me or forsake me. You are always there, and I don't have to worry about You ever leaving me. I can trust that You will walk with me all the days of my life. In Jesus' name, I pray. Amen.

Transformed by Love - Healing the Issues of the Heart

Day 29 - Letting Go and Walking in Forgiveness

> Instead, be kind to each other, tender-hearted, forgiving one another, just as God through Christ has forgiven you.
>
> Ephesians 4:32 (NLT)

Forgiveness is the decision to no longer carry resentment toward a person who has caused you harm. It is willingly choosing to let go of all the negativity and hurt caused by the offence. All feelings of pain, anger, and maybe even vengeance are gone. Sometimes we think that we have forgiven someone only to see them again and feel like we are back at square one. Recently, an ex-boyfriend messaged me on social media, and immediately some not-so-good words and feelings came up. The first was, "How dare he think he can just walk back into my life all casually after what he did to me!" I wanted to message him back with cruel words and let him know exactly how he made me feel. It was like I was the same woman from over ten years ago when I dealt with that heartbreak. I had to examine my heart, forgive once again, and choose to let it go even if he never apologized or understood the depth of my heartbreak. I decided not to respond, but to take those feelings to God and deal with the unforgiveness. In the end, I was thankful for the message because it revealed what was in my heart.

Forgiveness can sometimes be a gradual thing. For instance, you could have a dream about someone, and in the dream, you feel those grudges come up - the very feelings of unforgiveness you thought you had released. There were many people I had to forgive throughout my life, especially when I came to Christ. I learned to use this scenario as a gauge when it comes to forgiveness, I'm not sure where I learned it from or who said it first, but I use it often to ensure that I'm walking in forgiveness. If the person who hurt you walked into the room right now, how would you feel? Would those old feelings of anger and resentment come out? Would you feel awkward? Would you get up and walk out? Would you start telling them off? Would your guard go up?

Transformed by Love – Healing the Issues of the Heart

Day 29 – Letting Go and Walking in Forgiveness

> Instead, be kind to each other, tender-hearted, forgiving one another, just as God through Christ has forgiven you.
>
> Ephesians 4:32 (NLT)

Forgiveness is powerful. It is a beautiful gift from God that He first extended to us so that we could give it to others. Focusing on the fact that Christ went to the cross and forgave us, and completely washed our sins away, makes it much easier for me to forgive, over and over again, if need be. I want to honour Jesus and what He did for me by continuously extending my forgiveness just as He did for me. Without the forgiveness of God, I would still be entangled in darkness. Forgiveness offers me a relationship with the One, true God of Heaven and Earth.

You can still forgive even if you never receive an apology or get to tell the person how much they hurt you. Real forgiveness has no strings attached and it doesn't always mean there will be reconciliation. And you must be okay with that. When you choose to let go and live free from the burden of unforgiveness, you will not only be able to retain your peace and joy, but your heart will be strengthened. Your whole being will feel the release of unforgiveness, and your mind, body, and soul will prosper.

Transformed by Love - Healing the Issues of the Heart

Day 29 - Letting Go and Walking in Forgiveness

> Instead, be kind to each other, tender-hearted, forgiving one another, just as God through Christ has forgiven you.
>
> Ephesians 4:32 (NLT)

Your thoughts...

A Prayer for Forgiveness

Thank You, Lord, for forgiving my sins; in return, I can forgive others who have hurt me. Help me to let go and forgive, even when it's hard, and even in those times when I have to do it over and over. Thank You for the beautiful gift of forgiveness. I pray that You will help me keep my heart pure in all the things I do, and in all the relationships I have. As I choose to forgive, please heal my heart from all the repercussions of unforgiveness. Thank You for making my body, soul, and mind whole because I have released forgiveness. In Jesus' name, I pray. Amen.

Transformed by Love – Healing the Issues of the Heart
Day 30 – Guard Your Heart

Guard your heart above all else, for it determines the course of your life.
Proverbs 4:23 (NLT)

We are responsible for what we allow in our hearts. When unfair things happen to us, there are two possible outcomes. We determine if we will be bitter, unforgiving, and offended, or we can forgive, love, and allow God to work out His will in our situations. That's why this Scripture tells us to guard our hearts. The responsibility doesn't fall on God to protect our hearts – it falls on us. The Bible gives us direction on dealing with every hard thing that comes our way, but it is up to us to submit to what the Word says. If we decide that we are going to trust in God and His Word, then the course of our lives will continue to be blessed. But if we don't heed His Word, there will be consequences.

In Matthew 26, Jesus predicted two things about a couple of His disciples at the last supper. He told of Judas' betrayal and that Peter would deny Him three times. This painted a perfect picture of what we can do when we mess up. Judas betrayed Jesus and handed Him over to be arrested. Afterwards, he was so tormented that he took his own life. The night after Jesus was arrested, Peter went into town, and the people recognized him as one of Jesus' disciples. Fearful for his life, Peter denied knowing Jesus three times. The difference between Judas and Peter is that Peter was restored to the "course of life" that Jesus had for him. Judas, however, did not guard his heart but allowed greed to come in and accepted a monetary reward for the betrayal of Jesus. His "course of life" ended there. As for Peter, he went on to do great things for Christ, even though he had messed up. I believe Peter guarded his heart. He could have continued down the road of destruction as Judas did, but instead, he chose to keep his heart pure. I'm sure Peter not only accepted the forgiveness of Christ for what he did, but he also forgave himself. He kept his heart pure and continued

Transformed by Love – Healing the Issues of the Heart
Day 30 – Guard Your Heart

> Guard your heart above all else, for it determines the course of your life.
> Proverbs 4:23 (NLT)

doing great things for Jesus.

Guarding our hearts is a day-to-day responsibility. When we learn to make choices that keep our hearts pure, we can continue enjoying the peace and joy of God. Once God heals us from the pain of our past, we must continue to guard our hearts throughout our lives. We will always face circumstances that try and take us off God's course for us, but we need to choose to stay on track, even if we don't always make perfect decisions. God will restore us when we mess up; what matters is that we don't allow anything to take root in our hearts.

Since serving the Lord, I have been hurt many times. I also know I may have hurt others by what I said or did. But in the end, we all have the responsibility to keep our hearts pure. Sometimes, we may make the wrong decision and get off course, but we can choose to get back on track because God's grace and mercy are always available to us. Choose to guard your heart and keep it pure no matter what. Be watchful of what is taking place in your heart. Continue to check and ensure your heart is pure toward God and others. When you do that, you will succeed in staying the course and guarding what is so precious to God - your heart.

Transformed by Love – Healing the Issues of the Heart
Day 30 – Guard Your Heart

> Guard your heart above all else, for it determines the course of your life.
> Proverbs 4:23 (NLT)

Your thoughts...

A Prayer for Guarding Your Heart

Father, I pray that you will continue to help me guard my heart so that I can stay on the course You have for me. I will choose Your will and Your way every day and keep my heart pure. Lord, when I mess up, help me pick myself up, receive Your forgiveness, and continue walking with You. I will be diligent in guarding my heart against sin and will always submit to the Word of God. In Jesus' name. Amen.

Northern Initiative

Roberta Fiddler

Roberta grew up in the First Nations community of Waterhen Lake, located in Northern Saskatchewan, Canada. There were many obstacles and layers of oppression, which resulted in tremendous hurt. Deep-rooted healing needed to occur in her life after she came to Christ. She has experienced what she considers the typical life of an Indigenous person in Canada. As a second-generation residential school survivor, she experienced great difficulties in her childhood, such as abuse and neglect. Growing up in an alcoholic home, she witnessed constant domestic violence, faced poverty, struggled with low self-worth, and much more. Roberta once had a grim, hopeless view of the future, battling with the pain she carried from her past. It wasn't until she surrendered her heart to Jesus that He began to shape her and mould her into His new creation. Now she has a new life filled with hope, restoration, and beauty. Currently, she lives an abundant life as a mother, teacher, and mentor to many. She desires to bring inner, deep-rooted healing to others by sharing her real-life experiences. God has

Northern Initiative

About the Author

given Roberta a revelation on how to receive healing for your inner man and protect your mind, soul, and heart from the attacks of the enemy. She desires to share her stories of victory with you through this 30-day devotional. May these truths bring healing to your mind, soul, and heart as you read these words from Roberta's heart.

"Don't be afraid, for I am with you. Don't be discouraged, for I am your God. I will strengthen you and help you. I will hold you up with my victorious right hand."
Isaiah 41:10 (NLT)